Seisan   Kata Ana
Naifanchi Bunaki
Kusanku   Isshin-ryu   Seiunchin   Niseishi   Seipai
Chatanyara Kushanku   Shito-ryu   Ninjutsu   Sanchin
Bassai-Sho   Sunsu   Kempo   Jyuroku   Naihanchi
Goju-ryu   Seison   Gojushiho   Seiuchin   Wankan
Tensho   Enpi   Fukyugata   Bunkai
Heian   Kung F   esan   Passai-Dai
Kata   Naihan   inpei   Wanshu
Unsu   Sanka   Karate   Chinte
Seiryu   Kanku-   Pinan   Sochin
Hangetsu   Bunka   Jusan   Seiyunchin

Kata   Happiken   Naifanchin   Wado-ryu   Shimpa
Tae Kwon Do   Empi   Unshu   Gankaku   Martial Arts
Shisochin   Kushanku   Gensei-ryu   Sanseiru   Jiin
Kururunfu   Sanseru   Pechurin   Bunkai   Naihanchen
Nipaipo   Sanzhan   Taikyoku   Seisan   Kata Ananku
Wansu   Seishan   Annan   Naifanchi   Bunaki   Chinto
Annanko   Meikyo   Jitte   Kusanku   Isshin-ryu
Seiunchin   Niseishi   Seipai   Chatanyara Kushanku
Shito-ryu   Ninjutsu   Sanchin   Bassai-Sho   Sunsu
Kempo   Jyuroku   Naihanchi   Goju-ryu   Seison
Gojushiho   Seiuchin   Wankan   Tensho   Enpi   Jion
Rohai   Fukyugata   Bunkai   Heian   Kung Fu   Saifa
Ryuko   Sesan   Passai-Dai   Kata   Naihanchin
Shotokan   Suparinpei   Wanshu   Unsu   Sankakutobi
Shorin-ryu   Karate   Chinte   Seiryu   Kanku-dai
Tekki   Shuri-ryu   Pinan   Sochin   Hangetsu   Bunkai
Seienchin   Jusan   Seiyunchin   Kata   Happiken
Naifanchin   Wado-ryu   Shimpa   Tae Kwon Do   Empi
Unshu   Gankaku   Martial Arts   Shisochin   Kushanku
Gensei-ryu   Sanseiru   Jiin   Kururunfu   Sanseru
Pechurin   Bunkai   Naihanchen   Nipaipo   Sanzhan
Taikyoku   Seisan   Kata Ananku   Wansu   Seishan
Annan   Naifanchi   Bunaki   Chinto   Annanko   Meikyo
Jitte   Kusanku   Isshin-ryu   Seiunchin   Niseishi   Jiin

KATA APPLICATION NOTEBOOKS

ISSHINRYU
KARATE

Isshinryu Karate

ISBN-10: 061575385X
ISBN-13: 978-0615753850

https://www.createspace.com/4127249

Give feedback on this book at
BunkaiPress@hotmail.com

Printed in the U.S.A.

KATA APPLICATION NOTEBOOKS

ISSHINRYU
KARATE

Scott Britt

The Journal for Recording Kata
Applications and Bunkai

More in the Kata Application series:

This is the first in a series of notebooks – keep a look out for additional styles to be added!

Also coming soon - <u>The Isshinryu Bunkai Encyclopedia!</u>
See page 208 for more details.

Acknowledgments

My thanks to those that helped me get this notebook together – to my wife Mindy, my mother Laurie, my grandmother Lovelle, my karate students for their constant encouragement and proofreading, and to my aunt Dr. Susan Fritts for her professional editing services – this would not have been possible without their help.

My thanks also go to those who inspired me to create this book through their dedication to the traditional martial arts and the teaching of Bunkai. First and foremost to my teacher Keith Cofer, for planting a lifelong passion for karate in me, and for serving as a role model and father to me. Second, thanks are due to those that have served to spread the study of Bunkai – in particular, Pete Mills, Michael Garner, and Ian Abernathy.

Table of Contents

About the Author

At the time of this writing, Scott Britt is a 4th degree black belt in Isshinryu karate, and also holds rank in Shotokan, Agedo, and Kendo. In 2004, he was inducted into the United States Martial Arts Hall of Fame as "Bunkai Instructor of The Year." He has been an avid competitor, serving on the U.S. team in the 2004 World Games in Athens, Greece, where he brought home several medals in various divisions. He was also the 2004 and 2005 U.S. National Martial Arts Team Alliance "National Points Champion." In 2012, he was honored to join a team of martial artists going on a missions trip to the Ukraine, where they used their skills and talents to reach others for God.

Scott teaches karate in Oak Ridge, TN, and has a day job as an Instrumentation and Controls engineer. He and his wife Mindy, and 1-yr old son Leo (who already has his own Gi!), live in Spring City, TN. He views karate not as a hobby or as a part-time job, but as a calling and a ministry to help those who are weak become better able to defend themselves, to teach Christian values, and to introduce Christ to those who otherwise may never have had the opportunity to know Him.

Introduction

This Kata Applications Notebook (or "Bunkai Journal") is intended to help both the novice and advanced practitioner of karate alike to study in depth the applications and meaning behind the movements in their kata. It is a compact, yet comprehensive, tool for recording fighting techniques in an easily understood and quickly transcribed format.

Every kata has gems of knowledge and fighting application waiting to be extracted, techniques that go far beyond the basic "block-punch" taught in most schools today. This book in your hands is the result of my own search for hidden principles in kata – too many times have I sat at a seminar, trying desperately to write down not only a bunkai, but enough wording so that later I would know from which part of the kata it was supposed to come. And by then the speaker would have already moved on to his next point, leaving me hopelessly behind. And just as bad, when you have multiple sheets of such scribbled notes, from all different kata, how do you consolidate it into an understandable format once you get back home? After a three-day seminar, you are only going to have the faintest memory of what you were shown the first day.

It was on one such day – as I was attending Karate College in Richmond, VA – that I hit upon the idea for this notebook. I was frantically writing notes on a pad at the end of a full day of seminars taught by world-famous martial artists. Suddenly I thought, "What if my pad already had step-by-step photos of each kata?" Then I could flip to the place the instructor was talking about and make my notes, and I would never have to wonder where in the kata the

Bunkai was supposed to be applied. It would not only cut my writing time to a third of what it had been, but would also provide a permanent medium for recording all of my kata applications.

I have been using a draft version of this book for several years now, and it has served me very well. I hope students of Isshinryu everywhere will get the same benefit out of it that I have, and that it serves to deepen and strengthen their knowledge of the Isshinryu style.

What is Bunkai?

To put it simply, Bunkai means "Application" – specifically, the application of (or meaning behind) the movements found in traditional karate katas (or "Forms").

There are various types of Bunkai – there is the standard Bunkai, where the kata is taken at face value. This is where many schools of karate in America stop – "you step forward and punch the attacker in the stomach."

Then there is the Bunkai Oyo, the basic principles behind the kata. Dumping an opponent over your right leg followed by an elbow break may not exactly be in the kata move for move, but it uses the same underlying principles, combining moves from different parts of the kata and similar body positioning in relation to your opponent. This can be taught as a two-person drill, where the correct principles are used, but the kata may or may not be performed in the same original sequence.

Lastly there is Okuden waza, or "hidden techniques," in kata. Historically, Asian martial arts were taught from the teacher to a small handful of students in a manner that would better fit the description of an apprenticeship than a school. Many of the great masters never had karate dojos as we think of them today, with store fronts and signs with an agreement to teach anyone who wanted to learn for a monthly fee. They hand-picked their students, choosing only those with pure motives and the greatest desire to learn. Even then they did not just throw everything at them at once – they heavily drilled the basics at first, and slowly over the course of years entrusted their students with the deeper secrets of the style as they had the ability to understand them. Thus it might be that only a teacher's top student, or one who had been chosen as the successor to be head over a style (usually a member of the family, often the oldest son), would be entrusted with all of the secrets and hidden techniques within that style. Sadly, there have been instances where a teacher died prematurely, and some of the higher knowledge was lost.

Now that Bunkai has been defined, let's look at kata as a whole. With the high percentage of illiteracy in ancient China and Okinawa, the system of using kata to pass down fighting techniques was adapted as an effective means to ensure that a style would endure with minimal "loss of fidelity" through the generations. The katas are the record of the techniques and strategies for a style – thus, katas are not part of a style, they *are* the style. As a prime example, the kata Chinto was not always just one kata of many in the Isshinryu system – Chinto kata was the record of the fighting style of a man called Chinto, a Chinese sailor who was shipwrecked on the island of Okinawa sometime in the early 19th century.

All the katas in Isshinryu are similar – they all started as stand-alone entities, originating from different people, places, and time periods before being combined by various masters of Shuri-Te, and eventually Tatsuo Shimabuku under the common banner of Isshinryu Karate in 1956.

How to study Kata

When asking how to train in Kata, you are basically asking how to train in Bunkai. There are several different levels of training, which I have outlined below, that take a Kata from being a static, boring routine to being fully practical for real life self-defense.

1. **Solo Kata practice.** This is the bottom rung, the most basic and elementary level of practice. This is where you learn to copy the movements of your instructor, practicing against air. If you are blessed with a good instructor, he or she will also teach you the Bunkai or applications of the kata, though at this point it is still just "head knowledge" – not yet practical. While rote repetition is the initial form of training, it should not be neglected. The repetition and refining of the basic movements will enable you to create a foundation to build upon in later training.

2. **Two person drills.** This is where you get a training partner (or "Uke") and practice a particular Bunkai until you are proficient in it. As you slowly get better, you can increase the level of training by increasing speed and level of contact. You are well along the road to mastery if you can perform the technique against a "bad Uke," or a partner that resists and does not let you apply the technique on them right away.

3. **Kata against live opponents.** This is a fun form of training – one person starts in the middle with four training partners around him. Bowing in, he starts

running the kata exactly as he would in solo Kata practice. In this case, however, each time he turns there is a real opponent who provides a target for him to strike to, and to throw punches/strikes for him to block. The same guidelines for making the drill more difficult from #2 apply here as well.

4. **Kata based one-step sparring.** This activity is where it starts getting more realistic. Standing across from your partner, take turns delivering a single attack, that must then be defended against using a technique from kata. Starting out, you may limit the number of possible attacks to three or four, and then as you progress increase the number so that your partner is never quite sure what defence he would need to use.

5. **Kata based sparring.** This is the height of kata training – you and your partner have a sparring match, where you can only defend yourself using techniques from kata! Not only do you not know what technique is coming next, but you have a very non-compliant partner. This is not the time to stop and think about what you are going to do – this is where you find out the effectiveness of your previous training, and if you have indeed drilled the Bunkai into your muscle memory so that it has become a matter of instinct. Because of the need to allow grabs and takedowns, no pads are used in this training. This will necessitate light to non-contact sparring among the lower belts and reasonable caution among the upper belts.

There have been some martial artists who have turned their backs on kata, saying that kata are not practical. And considering the way many schools teach kata, they would be right! Many schools only teach kata as a requirement for the next belt, and rarely teach what the individual moves are for, let alone provide training with a partner on the individual Bunkai. But this is what is required to make your kata practical – an in-depth study of the meaning behind the moves, followed up by training with a partner to drill the Bunkai into your muscle memory. The katas have so much to teach us – do not let this wealth of information go undiscovered!

How to use this book

This notebook is set up so that with just a few quick marks at the start of a cell, you can be on your way to recording Bunkai. The cells are set up to allow you to record lots of information in a small space, but you do not have to use all of the areas – just fill in the fields that you think would be a help to your study. See below for a diagram of how the cells are set up:

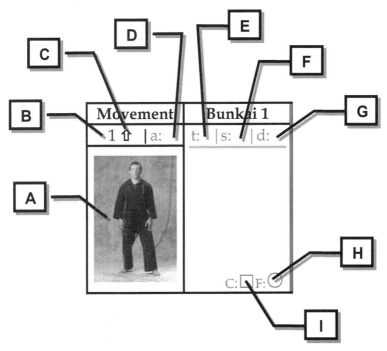

A. **Photo** of the particular move in the kata. *See page 8.*
B. **Kata movement number. (1, 2, etc.)**
C. **Direction arrow. (⇑)** Looking down from above, this indicates where you are facing during that move in the kata. Arrow pointing downward is the starting position (bow in). *See page 8.*
D. **Additional Bunkai. (a:)** If you fill up all three Bunkai columns for a particular movement, you can add

additional Bunkai in Appendix A. Put a check mark in this square so you know there is more to be found in the back.

E. **Type. (t:)** Here you can enter what type of Bunkai this is, such as G for grappling, J for joint lock, etc. A full list of types, along with blanks to record your own, can be found in Appendix G.

F. **Source. (s:)** This field allows you to enter a number to indicate where you got this Bunkai from – your instructor, a seminar, etc. Simply enter your source in Appendix F at the back of the book, and then use that reference number any time you write down a Bunkai from that source.

G. **Difficulty. (d:)** This space allows you to enter the difficulty rating for the Bunkai, on a scale of 1-4. In other words, how hard is it to master? Is it intuitive? See Appendix G for a breakdown of the difficulty ranges.

H. **Finished. (F:O)** Fill in this circle when you are at the end of a Bunkai.

I. **Continued. (C:☒)** Check this box when the Bunkai is continued into the next cell below. Most Bunkai will take up several moves in a kata, and thus several cells.

Abbreviations:

It makes sense to use abbreviations, like a sort of Martial Arts shorthand, when writing down Bunkai in a seminar setting. For instance, instead of writing:

"Opponent throws a right hand punch. Step back with right foot and grab opponents right hand with my left hand, then punch opponent in face with left hand."

It makes more sense to write something like this:

"OP throws RH P. Step B with RF and GB OP's RH with my LH. P to OP face with LH."

See Appendix H for a list of suggested abbreviations, along with blank spaces to write your own.

NOTES:

While this book includes photos and descriptions of each kata movement, these are not intended to teach Kata but to serve as a reference for recording your own observations and applications. This journal assumes you have at least a basic knowledge of the kata on which you are making notes at the time - refer to your teacher for learning kata movements. The intent of the photos is to match as closely as possible Tatsuo's 1964 and 1966 films; any personal interpretation perceived as coming from the author is completely unintentional.

The photos of each movement are taken from the best angle, and not necessarily from the direction faced at the beginning of the kata. To tell which direction is being faced in the kata, refer to the arrow next to the movement number. See diagram below for an illustration looking down from above:

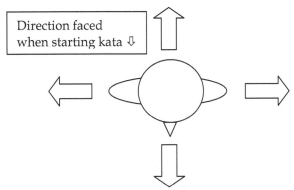

Direction faced when starting kata ⇩

Ready for an example of all this put together? See the next page!

EXAMPLE:

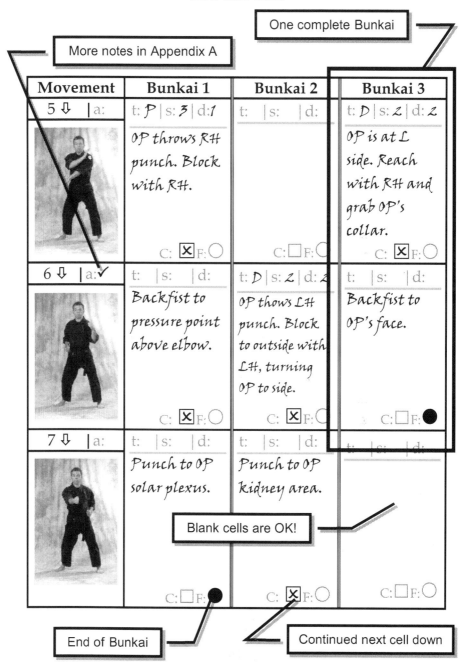

One complete Bunkai

More notes in Appendix A

Movement	Bunkai 1	Bunkai 2	Bunkai 3
5 ⇩	a:	t: P	s: 3	d: 1 OP throws RH punch. Block with RH. C: ☒ F: ◯	t:	s:	d: C: ☐ F: ◯	t: D	s: 2	d: 2 OP is at L side. Reach with RH and grab OP's collar. C: ☒ F: ◯
6 ⇩	a: ✔	t:	s:	d: Backfist to pressure point above elbow. C: ☒ F: ◯	t: D	s: 2	d: 2 OP thows LH punch. Block to outside with LH, turning OP to side. C: ☒ F: ◯	t:	s:	d: Backfist to OP's face. C: ☐ F: ●
7 ⇩	a:	t:	s:	d: Punch to OP solar plexus. C: ☐ F: ●	t:	s:	d: Punch to OP kidney area. C: ☒ F: ◯	t:	s:	d: C: ☐ F: ◯

Blank cells are OK!

End of Bunkai

Continued next cell down

Seisan
Kata

Note: Photos were taken at an angle that shows each movement best – refer to arrows for direction faced in that particular movement. See "Note" on page 8.

Movement	Bunkai 1	Bunkai 2	Bunkai 3
1 ⇩ |a:	t: |s: |d:	t: |s: |d:	t: |s: |d:
	C:☐ F:◯	C:☐ F:◯	C:☐ F:◯
2⇩ |a:	t: |s: |d:	t: |s: |d:	t: |s: |d:
	C:☐ F:◯	C:☐ F:◯	C:☐ F:◯
3⇩ |a:	t: |s: |d:	t: |s: |d:	t: |s: |d:
	C:☐ F:◯	C:☐ F:◯	C:☐ F:◯
4⇩ |a:	t: |s: |d:	t: |s: |d:	t: |s: |d:
	C:☐ F:◯	C:☐ F:◯	C:☐ F:◯

Movement	Bunkai 1	Bunkai 2	Bunkai 3
5⇩ |a:	t: |s: |d: C:☐ F:◯	t: |s: |d: C:☐ F:◯	t: |s: |d: C:☐ F:◯
6⇩ |a:	t: |s: |d: C:☐ F:◯	t: |s: |d: C:☐ F:◯	t: |s: |d: C:☐ F:◯
7⇩ |a:	t: |s: |d: C:☐ F:◯	t: |s: |d: C:☐ F:◯	t: |s: |d: C:☐ F:◯
8⇩ |a:	t: |s: |d: C:☐ F:◯	t: |s: |d: C:☐ F:◯	t: |s: |d: C:☐ F:◯

Seisan

Movement	Bunkai 1	Bunkai 2	Bunkai 3
9⇩ |a:	t: |s: |d: c:☐ f:○	t: |s: |d: c:☐ f:○	t: |s: |d: c:☐ f:○
10⇩ |a:	t: |s: |d: c:☐ f:○	t: |s: |d: c:☐ f:○	t: |s: |d: c:☐ f:○
11⇩ |a:	t: |s: |d: c:☐ f:○	t: |s: |d: c:☐ f:○	t: |s: |d: c:☐ f:○
12⇧ |a:	t: |s: |d: c:☐ f:○	t: |s: |d: c:☐ f:○	t: |s: |d: c:☐ f:○

Movement	Bunkai 1	Bunkai 2	Bunkai 3
13⇧ | a:	t: | s: | d:	t: | s: | d:	t: | s: | d:
	C:☐ F:◯	C:☐ F:◯	C:☐ F:◯
14⇧ | a:	t: | s: | d:	t: | s: | d:	t: | s: | d:
	C:☐ F:◯	C:☐ F:◯	C:☐ F:◯
15⇧ | a:	t: | s: | d:	t: | s: | d:	t: | s: | d:
	C:☐ F:◯	C:☐ F:◯	C:☐ F:◯
16⇧ | a:	t: | s: | d:	t: | s: | d:	t: | s: | d:
	C:☐ F:◯	C:☐ F:◯	C:☐ F:◯

Movement	Bunkai 1	Bunkai 2	Bunkai 3
17⇧ |a:	t: |s: |d:	t: |s: |d:	t: |s: |d:
	C:☐F:◯	C:☐F:◯	C:☐F:◯
18⇧ |a:	t: |s: |d:	t: |s: |d:	t: |s: |d:
	C:☐F:◯	C:☐F:◯	C:☐F:◯
19⇧ |a:	t: |s: |d:	t: |s: |d:	t: |s: |d:
	C:☐F:◯	C:☐F:◯	C:☐F:◯
20⇧ |a:	t: |s: |d:	t: |s: |d:	t: |s: |d:
	C:☐F:◯	C:☐F:◯	C:☐F:◯

Movement	Bunkai 1	Bunkai 2	Bunkai 3
21 ⇧ | a:	t:　|s:　|d:	t:　|s:　|d:	t:　|s:　|d:
	C:☐F:◯	C:☐F:◯	C:☐F:◯
22⇧ | a:	t:　|s:　|d:	t:　|s:　|d:	t:　|s:　|d:
	C:☐F:◯	C:☐F:◯	C:☐F:◯
23⇧ | a:	t:　|s:　|d:	t:　|s:　|d:	t:　|s:　|d:
	C:☐F:◯	C:☐F:◯	C:☐F:◯
24⇐ | a:	t:　|s:　|d:	t:　|s:　|d:	t:　|s:　|d:
	C:☐F:◯	C:☐F:◯	C:☐F:◯

Movement	Bunkai 1	Bunkai 2	Bunkai 3
25⇐ |a:	t: |s: |d: C:☐ F:○	t: |s: |d: C:☐ F:○	t: |s: |d: C:☐ F:○
26⇐ |a:	t: |s: |d: C:☐ F:○	t: |s: |d: C:☐ F:○	t: |s: |d: C:☐ F:○
27⇐ |a:	t: |s: |d: C:☐ F:○	t: |s: |d: C:☐ F:○	t: |s: |d: C:☐ F:○
28⇐ |a:	t: |s: |d: C:☐ F:○	t: |s: |d: C:☐ F:○	t: |s: |d: C:☐ F:○

Movement	Bunkai 1	Bunkai 2	Bunkai 3
29⇧ |a:	t: |s: |d:	t: |s: |d:	t: |s: |d:
	C:☐ F:◯	C:☐ F:◯	C:☐ F:◯
30⇨ |a:	t: |s: |d:	t: |s: |d:	t: |s: |d:
	C:☐ F:◯	C:☐ F:◯	C:☐ F:◯
31⇨ |a:	t: |s: |d:	t: |s: |d:	t: |s: |d:
	C:☐ F:◯	C:☐ F:◯	C:☐ F:◯
32⇨ |a:	t: |s: |d:	t: |s: |d:	t: |s: |d:
	C:☐ F:◯	C:☐ F:◯	C:☐ F:◯

Movement	Bunkai 1	Bunkai 2	Bunkai 3
33⇨ |a:	t: |s: |d: C:☐F:○	t: |s: |d: C:☐F:○	t: |s: |d: C:☐F:○
34⇨ |a:	t: |s: |d: C:☐F:○	t: |s: |d: C:☐F:○	t: |s: |d: C:☐F:○
35⇨ |a:	t: |s: |d: C:☐F:○	t: |s: |d: C:☐F:○	t: |s: |d: C:☐F:○
36⇧ |a:	t: |s: |d: C:☐F:○	t: |s: |d: C:☐F:○	t: |s: |d: C:☐F:○

Movement	Bunkai 1	Bunkai 2	Bunkai 3
37⇧ |a:	t: |s: |d: C:☐ F:○	t: |s: |d: C:☐ F:○	t: |s: |d: C:☐ F:○
38⇧ |a:	t: |s: |d: C:☐ F:○	t: |s: |d: C:☐ F:○	t: |s: |d: C:☐ F:○
39⇧ |a:	t: |s: |d: C:☐ F:○	t: |s: |d: C:☐ F:○	t: |s: |d: C:☐ F:○
40⇧ |a:	t: |s: |d: C:☐ F:○	t: |s: |d: C:☐ F:○	t: |s: |d: C:☐ F:○

21

Movement	Bunkai 1	Bunkai 2	Bunkai 3
41 ⇧ |a:	t: |s: |d:	t: |s: |d:	t: |s: |d:
	C:☐ F:◯	C:☐ F:◯	C:☐ F:◯
42⇧ |a:	t: |s: |d:	t: |s: |d:	t: |s: |d:
	C:☐ F:◯	C:☐ F:◯	C:☐ F:◯
43⇩ |a:	t: |s: |d:	t: |s: |d:	t: |s: |d:
	C:☐ F:◯	C:☐ F:◯	C:☐ F:◯
44⇩ |a:	t: |s: |d:	t: |s: |d:	t: |s: |d:
	C:☐ F:◯	C:☐ F:◯	C:☐ F:◯

Movement	Bunkai 1	Bunkai 2	Bunkai 3
45⇩ |a:	t: |s: |d: C:☐ F:○	t: |s: |d: C:☐ F:○	t: |s: |d: C:☐ F:○
46⇩ |a:	t: |s: |d: C:☐ F:○	t: |s: |d: C:☐ F:○	t: |s: |d: C:☐ F:○
47⇩ |a:	t: |s: |d: C:☐ F:○	t: |s: |d: C:☐ F:○	t: |s: |d: C:☐ F:○
48⇩ |a:	t: |s: |d: C:☐ F:○	t: |s: |d: C:☐ F:○	t: |s: |d: C:☐ F:○

Movement	Bunkai 1	Bunkai 2	Bunkai 3
49⇩ |a:	t: |s: |d:	t: |s: |d:	t: |s: |d:
	C:☐ F:◯	C:☐ F:◯	C:☐ F:◯
50⇩ |a:	t: |s: |d:	t: |s: |d:	t: |s: |d:
	C:☐ F:◯	C:☐ F:◯	C:☐ F:◯
51⇧ |a:	t: |s: |d:	t: |s: |d:	t: |s: |d:
	C:☐ F:◯	C:☐ F:◯	C:☐ F:◯
52⇧ |a:	t: |s: |d:	t: |s: |d:	t: |s: |d:
	C:☐ F:◯	C:☐ F:◯	C:☐ F:◯

Movement	Bunkai 1	Bunkai 2	Bunkai 3
53⇧ |a:	t: |s: |d:	t: |s: |d:	t: |s: |d:
	C:☐ F:○	C:☐ F:○	C:☐ F:○
54⇧ |a:	t: |s: |d:	t: |s: |d:	t: |s: |d:
	C:☐ F:○	C:☐ F:○	C:☐ F:○
55⇧ |a:	t: |s: |d:	t: |s: |d:	t: |s: |d:
	C:☐ F:○	C:☐ F:○	C:☐ F:○
56⇧ |a:	t: |s: |d:	t: |s: |d:	t: |s: |d:
	C:☐ F:○	C:☐ F:○	C:☐ F:○

Movement	Bunkai 1	Bunkai 2	Bunkai 3
57⇧ |a:	t: |s: |d: c:☐ f:◯	t: |s: |d: c:☐ f:◯	t: |s: |d: c:☐ f:◯
58⇧ |a:	t: |s: |d: c:☐ f:◯	t: |s: |d: c:☐ f:◯	t: |s: |d: c:☐ f:◯
59⇩ |a:	t: |s: |d: c:☐ f:◯	t: |s: |d: c:☐ f:◯	t: |s: |d: c:☐ f:◯
60⇩ |a:	t: |s: |d: c:☐ f:◯	t: |s: |d: c:☐ f:◯	t: |s: |d: c:☐ f:◯

Movement	Bunkai 1	Bunkai 2	Bunkai 3
61 ⇩ |a:	t: |s: |d: C:☐F:◯	t: |s: |d: C:☐F:◯	t: |s: |d: C:☐F:◯
62⇩ |a:	t: |s: |d: C:☐F:◯	t: |s: |d: C:☐F:◯	t: |s: |d: C:☐F:◯
63⇩|a:	t: |s: |d: C:☐F:◯	t: |s: |d: C:☐F:◯	t: |s: |d: C:☐F:◯
64⇩ |a:	t: |s: |d: C:☐F:◯	t: |s: |d: C:☐F:◯	t: |s: |d: C:☐F:◯

27

Movement	Bunkai 1	Bunkai 2	Bunkai 3
65⇩ |a:	t: |s: |d:	t: |s: |d:	t: |s: |d:
	C:☐ F:◯	C:☐ F:◯	C:☐ F:◯
66⇩ |a:	t: |s: |d:	t: |s: |d:	t: |s: |d:
	C:☐ F:◯	C:☐ F:◯	C:☐ F:◯
67⇩ |a:	t: |s: |d:	t: |s: |d:	t: |s: |d:
	C:☐ F:◯	C:☐ F:◯	C:☐ F:◯
68⇩ |a:	t: |s: |d:	t: |s: |d:	t: |s: |d:
	C:☐ F:◯	C:☐ F:◯	C:☐ F:◯

Movement	Bunkai 1	Bunkai 2	Bunkai 3
69⇩ |a:	t: |s: |d: C:☐ F:○	t: |s: |d: C:☐ F:○	t: |s: |d: C:☐ F:○
70⇩ |a:	t: |s: |d: C:☐ F:○	t: |s: |d: C:☐ F:○	t: |s: |d: C:☐ F:○
71⇩ |a:	t: |s: |d: C:☐ F:○	t: |s: |d: C:☐ F:○	t: |s: |d: C:☐ F:○
72⇩ |a:	t: |s: |d: C:☐ F:○	t: |s: |d: C:☐ F:○	t: |s: |d: C:☐ F:○

Movement	Bunkai 1	Bunkai 2	Bunkai 3
73⇩ |a:	t: |s: |d: C:☐F:◯	t: |s: |d: C:☐F:◯	t: |s: |d: C:☐F:◯
74⇩ |a:	t: |s: |d: C:☐F:◯	t: |s: |d: C:☐F:◯	t: |s: |d: C:☐F:◯
75⇩ |a:	t: |s: |d: C:☐F:◯	t: |s: |d: C:☐F:◯	t: |s: |d: C:☐F:◯

Seisan Breakdown

This section gives a brief explanation of each movement, following the numbering of the photos. Reminder - this is provided for reference only (see Note on page 8).

1. Stand at attention
2. Bow
3. Salutation
4. Ready stance
5. Step up left foot, prepare for…
6. Left side block
7. Right hand punch
8. Step up with right foot, left hand punch
9. Step up with left foot, right hand punch
10. Double-fist into center
11. Half-step forward, double head-blocks
12. X-block with 180° pivot
13. Double knife-hand downward strike
14. Step forward with right foot, right hand inverted ridge-hand
15. Turn right hand over
16. Pull elbow toward hip
17. Step forward with left foot, left hand inverted ridge-hand
18. Turn left hand over
19. Pull elbow toward hip
20. Step forward with right foot, right hand inverted ridge-hand
21. Turn right hand over

22. Pull elbow toward hip
23. Stack hands on right hip
24. Turn left, left hand side block
25. Right hand punch
26. Left hand punch
27. Right foot straight kick
28. Right hand punch
29. Stack hands on left hip
30. Turn 180° into Seisan stance, right hand side block
31. Left hand punch
32. Right hand punch
33. Left foot straight kick
34. Left hand punch
35. Stack hands on right hip
36. Turn left, left hand side block
37. Right hand punch
38. Left hand punch
39. Right foot straight kick
40. Right hand punch
41. Pivot right foot into Seiunchin stance
42. Squat block
43. Turn 180° and draw back
44. Step out, right hand bridge-of-nose strike
45. Draw back, drop right elbow
46. Step across with left foot
47. Right foot straight kick
48. Straighten into Seisan stance, right hand leg block
49. Left hand punch
50. Pivot left foot into Seiunchin stance, squat block

51. Turn 180° and draw back

52. Step out, left hand bridge-of-nose strike

53. Draw back, drop left elbow

54. Step across with right foot

55. Left foot straight kick

56. Straighten into Seisan stance, left hand leg block

57. Right hand punch

58. Pivot right foot into Seiunchin stance, squat block

59. Turn 180° and draw back

60. Step out, right hand bridge-of-nose strike

61. Straighten into Seisan stance, right hand leg block

62. Left hand punch

63. Pivot left foot into Seiunchin stance, squat block

64. Draw back into cat stance, left hand open arc sweep

65. Straighten into Seisan stance

66. Right foot straight kick

67. Right hand punch

68. Extend left hand to meet right hand

69. Draw back into cat stance

70. Bring arms in circle to hips

71. Right hand high, left hand low

72. Bring feet together…

73. Closing salutation

74. Bow

75. End of kata

Seiunchin
Kata

Note: Photos were taken at an angle that shows each movement best – refer to arrows for direction faced in that particular movement. See "Note" on page 8.

Movement	Bunkai 1	Bunkai 2	Bunkai 3
1 ⇩ |a:	t: |s: |d: C:☐ F:○	t: |s: |d: C:☐ F:○	t: |s: |d: C:☐ F:○
2 ⇩ |a:	t: |s: |d: C:☐ F:○	t: |s: |d: C:☐ F:○	t: |s: |d: C:☐ F:○
3 ⇩ |a:	t: |s: |d: C:☐ F:○	t: |s: |d: C:☐ F:○	t: |s: |d: C:☐ F:○
4 ⇩ |a:	t: |s: |d: C:☐ F:○	t: |s: |d: C:☐ F:○	t: |s: |d: C:☐ F:○

Movement	Bunkai 1	Bunkai 2	Bunkai 3
5⇨ |a:	t: |s: |d: C:☐F:◯	t: |s: |d: C:☐F:◯	t: |s: |d: C:☐F:◯
6⇨ |a:	t: |s: |d: C:☐F:◯	t: |s: |d: C:☐F:◯	t: |s: |d: C:☐F:◯
7⇨ |a:	t: |s: |d: C:☐F:◯	t: |s: |d: C:☐F:◯	t: |s: |d: C:☐F:◯
8⇨ |a:	t: |s: |d: C:☐F:◯	t: |s: |d: C:☐F:◯	t: |s: |d: C:☐F:◯

Movement	Bunkai 1	Bunkai 2	Bunkai 3
9⇨ |a:	t: |s: |d:	t: |s: |d:	t: |s: |d:
	c:☐ F:◯	c:☐ F:◯	c:☐ F:◯
10⇨ |a:	t: |s: |d:	t: |s: |d:	t: |s: |d:
	c:☐ F:◯	c:☐ F:◯	c:☐ F:◯
11⇦|a:	t: |s: |d:	t: |s: |d:	t: |s: |d:
	c:☐ F:◯	c:☐ F:◯	c:☐ F:◯
12⇦ |a:	t: |s: |d:	t: |s: |d:	t: |s: |d:
	c:☐ F:◯	c:☐ F:◯	c:☐ F:◯

Movement	Bunkai 1	Bunkai 2	Bunkai 3
13⇐ |a:	t: |s: |d: C:☐ F:◯	t: |s: |d: C:☐ F:◯	t: |s: |d: C:☐ F:◯
14⇐ |a:	t: |s: |d: C:☐ F:◯	t: |s: |d: C:☐ F:◯	t: |s: |d: C:☐ F:◯
15⇐ |a:	t: |s: |d: C:☐ F:◯	t: |s: |d: C:☐ F:◯	t: |s: |d: C:☐ F:◯
16⇐ |a:	t: |s: |d: C:☐ F:◯	t: |s: |d: C:☐ F:◯	t: |s: |d: C:☐ F:◯

Movement	Bunkai 1	Bunkai 2	Bunkai 3
17⇨ |a:	t:　|s:　|d: C:☐ F:○	t:　|s:　|d: C:☐ F:○	t:　|s:　|d: C:☐ F:○
18⇨ |a:	t:　|s:　|d: C:☐ F:○	t:　|s:　|d: C:☐ F:○	t:　|s:　|d: C:☐ F:○
19⇨ |a:	t:　|s:　|d: C:☐ F:○	t:　|s:　|d: C:☐ F:○	t:　|s:　|d: C:☐ F:○
20⇨ |a:	t:　|s:　|d: C:☐ F:○	t:　|s:　|d: C:☐ F:○	t:　|s:　|d: C:☐ F:○

Movement	Bunkai 1	Bunkai 2	Bunkai 3
21 ⇨ |a:	t: |s: |d: C:☐F:○	t: |s: |d: C:☐F:○	t: |s: |d: C:☐F:○
22⇨ |a:	t: |s: |d: C:☐F:○	t: |s: |d: C:☐F:○	t: |s: |d: C:☐F:○
23⇨ |a:	t: |s: |d: C:☐F:○	t: |s: |d: C:☐F:○	t: |s: |d: C:☐F:○
24⇩ |a:	t: |s: |d: C:☐F:○	t: |s: |d: C:☐F:○	t: |s: |d: C:☐F:○

Movement	Bunkai 1	Bunkai 2	Bunkai 3
25⇩ |a:	t: |s: |d: c:☐ f:○	t: |s: |d: c:☐ f:○	t: |s: |d: c:☐ f:○
26⇩ |a:	t: |s: |d: c:☐ f:○	t: |s: |d: c:☐ f:○	t: |s: |d: c:☐ f:○
27⇩ |a:	t: |s: |d: c:☐ f:○	t: |s: |d: c:☐ f:○	t: |s: |d: c:☐ f:○
28⇩ |a:	t: |s: |d: c:☐ f:○	t: |s: |d: c:☐ f:○	t: |s: |d: c:☐ f:○

Movement	Bunkai 1	Bunkai 2	Bunkai 3
29↙ |a:	t: |s: |d:	t: |s: |d:	t: |s: |d:
	C:☐ F:○	C:☐ F:○	C:☐ F:○
30↙ |a:	t: |s: |d:	t: |s: |d:	t: |s: |d:
	C:☐ F:○	C:☐ F:○	C:☐ F:○
31↙ |a:	t: |s: |d:	t: |s: |d:	t: |s: |d:
	C:☐ F:○	C:☐ F:○	C:☐ F:○
32↘ |a:	t: |s: |d:	t: |s: |d:	t: |s: |d:
	C:☐ F:○	C:☐ F:○	C:☐ F:○

43

Movement	Bunkai 1	Bunkai 2	Bunkai 3
33↘ |a:	t: |s: |d:	t: |s: |d:	t: |s: |d:
	C:☐ F:◯	C:☐ F:◯	C:☐ F:◯
34↘ |a:	t: |s: |d:	t: |s: |d:	t: |s: |d:
	C:☐ F:◯	C:☐ F:◯	C:☐ F:◯
35⇩ |a:	t: |s: |d:	t: |s: |d:	t: |s: |d:
	C:☐ F:◯	C:☐ F:◯	C:☐ F:◯
36⇩ |a:	t: |s: |d:	t: |s: |d:	t: |s: |d:
	C:☐ F:◯	C:☐ F:◯	C:☐ F:◯

Movement	Bunkai 1	Bunkai 2	Bunkai 3
37⇩ |a:	t: |s: |d: C:☐F:◯	t: |s: |d: C:☐F:◯	t: |s: |d: C:☐F:◯
38⇩ |a:	t: |s: |d: C:☐F:◯	t: |s: |d: C:☐F:◯	t: |s: |d: C:☐F:◯
39⇩ |a:	t: |s: |d: C:☐F:◯	t: |s: |d: C:☐F:◯	t: |s: |d: C:☐F:◯
40⇩ |a:	t: |s: |d: C:☐F:◯	t: |s: |d: C:☐F:◯	t: |s: |d: C:☐F:◯

Movement	Bunkai 1	Bunkai 2	Bunkai 3
41 ⇧ |a:	t: |s: |d:	t: |s: |d:	t: |s: |d:
	C:☐ F:◯	C:☐ F:◯	C:☐ F:◯
42↖ |a:	t: |s: |d:	t: |s: |d:	t: |s: |d:
	C:☐ F:◯	C:☐ F:◯	C:☐ F:◯
43↖ |a:	t: |s: |d:	t: |s: |d:	t: |s: |d:
	C:☐ F:◯	C:☐ F:◯	C:☐ F:◯
44↖ |a:	t: |s: |d:	t: |s: |d:	t: |s: |d:
	C:☐ F:◯	C:☐ F:◯	C:☐ F:◯

Movement	Bunkai 1	Bunkai 2	Bunkai 3
45 ↘ |a:	t: |s: |d: C:☐ F:○	t: |s: |d: C:☐ F:○	t: |s: |d: C:☐ F:○
46 ↘ |a:	t: |s: |d: C:☐ F:○	t: |s: |d: C:☐ F:○	t: |s: |d: C:☐ F:○
47 ↘ |a:	t: |s: |d: C:☐ F:○	t: |s: |d: C:☐ F:○	t: |s: |d: C:☐ F:○
48 ↘ |a:	t: |s: |d: C:☐ F:○	t: |s: |d: C:☐ F:○	t: |s: |d: C:☐ F:○

Movement	Bunkai 1	Bunkai 2	Bunkai 3
49 ꙍ | a:	t: | s: | d:	t: | s: | d: .	t: | s: | d:
	C:☐ F:◯	C:☐ F:◯	C:☐ F:◯
50 ꙍ | a:	t: | s: | d:	t: | s: | d:	t: | s: | d:
	C:☐ F:◯	C:☐ F:◯	C:☐ F:◯
51 ꙍ | a:	t: | s: | d:	t: | s: | d:	t: | s: | d:
	C:☐ F:◯	C:☐ F:◯	C:☐ F:◯
52 ꙍ | a:	t: | s: | d:	t: | s: | d:	t: | s: | d:
	C:☐ F:◯	C:☐ F:◯	C:☐ F:◯

Movement	Bunkai 1	Bunkai 2	Bunkai 3
53⇩ | a:	t: | s: | d: C:☐ F:◯	t: | s: | d: C:☐ F:◯	t: | s: | d: C:☐ F:◯
54⇩ | a:	t: | s: | d: C:☐ F:◯	t: | s: | d: C:☐ F:◯	t: | s: | d: C:☐ F:◯
55⇩ | a:	t: | s: | d: C:☐ F:◯	t: | s: | d: C:☐ F:◯	t: | s: | d: C:☐ F:◯
56⇩ | a:	t: | s: | d: C:☐ F:◯	t: | s: | d: C:☐ F:◯	t: | s: | d: C:☐ F:◯

49

Movement	Bunkai 1	Bunkai 2	Bunkai 3
57⇩ |a:	t: |s: |d: c:☐ f:○	t: |s: |d: c:☐ f:○	t: |s: |d: c:☐ f:○
58⇩ |a:	t: |s: |d: c:☐ f:○	t: |s: |d: c:☐ f:○	t: |s: |d: c:☐ f:○
59⇩ |a:	t: |s: |d: c:☐ f:○	t: |s: |d: c:☐ f:○	t: |s: |d: c:☐ f:○
60⇩ |a:	t: |s: |d: c:☐ f:○	t: |s: |d: c:☐ f:○	t: |s: |d: c:☐ f:○

Movement	Bunkai 1	Bunkai 2	Bunkai 3
61 ⇩ |a:	t: |s: |d:	t: |s: |d:	t: |s: |d:
	C:☐ F:◯	C:☐ F:◯	C:☐ F:◯
62⇩ |a:	t: |s: |d:	t: |s: |d:	t: |s: |d:
	C:☐ F:◯	C:☐ F:◯	C:☐ F:◯
63⇩|a:	t: |s: |d:	t: |s: |d:	t: |s: |d:
	C:☐ F:◯	C:☐ F:◯	C:☐ F:◯
64⇩ |a:	t: |s: |d:	t: |s: |d:	t: |s: |d:
	C:☐ F:◯	C:☐ F:◯	C:☐ F:◯

Seiunchin Breakdown

This section gives a brief explanation of each movement, following the numbering of the photos. Reminder - this is provided for reference only (see Note on page 8).

1. Stand at attention
2. Bow
3. Salutation
4. Ready stance
5. Turn left into Seiunchin stance
6. Bring both hands up in knife hand
7. Double hammerfist down
8. Right hand inverted ridgehand
9. Turn right hand over
10. Pull into gouge
11. Step up 180° into Seiunchin stance
12. Bring both hands up in knife hand
13. Double hammerfist down
14. Left hand inverted ridgehand
15. Turn left hand over
16. Pull into gouge
17. Step up 180° into Seiunchin stance
18. Bring both hands up in knife hand
19. Double hammerfist down
20. Right hand inverted ridgehand
21. Turn right hand over
22. Pull into gouge
23. Right hand backfist into left hand
24. Draw back into Seisan stance
25. Right hand reinforced punch
26. Drop right hand to belt
27. Right elbow into left hand

28. Left hand on right fist
29. Reinforced block on a 45° right
30. Step up on 45° in Seiunchin stance, leg block
31. Step back on 45° in Seiunchin stance, leg block
32. Reinforced block on a 45° left
33. Step up on 45° in Seiunchin stance, leg block
34. Step back on 45° in Seiunchin stance, leg block
35. Step back into Seiunchin stance, left arm over right
36. Right hand low block, left hand high block
37. Step back into Seiunchin stance, right arm over left
38. Left hand low block, right hand high block
39. Step up into Seisan stance, right forearm smash
40. Shuffle forwards, right hand bridge of nose strike
41. Pivot on heels 180°, high/low blocks
42. Right hand to chest, left foot up
43. Step out 45° to left in Seiunchin stance,left hand uppercut
44. Left hand backfist
45. Left hand leg block
46. Step back 180° in Seiunchin stance, right hand leg block
47. Pivot 180° on heels, high/low blocks
48. Left hand to chest, right foot up
49. Step out 45° to in Seiunchin stance,right hand uppercut
50. Right hand backfist
51. Right hand leg block
52. Step back 180° in Seiunchin stance, left hand leg block
53. Draw left foot behind into cat stance
54. Bearhug break
55. Draw right foot behind into cat stance
56. Bearhug break
57. Punch downward with right hand
58. Step up into Seisan, right hand backfist
59. Draw right foot back into crane stance

60. Draw arms in large circle, end with elbows close together
61. Stomp, draw down elbows
62. Draw up in attention
63. Closing salutation
64. Bow

Naihanchi Kata

Note: Photos were taken at an angle that shows each movement best – refer to arrows for direction faced in that particular movement. See "Note" on page 8.

Movement	Bunkai 1	Bunkai 2	Bunkai 3
1 ⇩ |a:	t: |s: |d:	t: |s: |d:	t: |s: |d:
	C:☐ F:○	C:☐ F:○	C:☐ F:○
2 ⇩ |a:	t: |s: |d:	t: |s: |d:	t: |s: |d:
	C:☐ F:○	C:☐ F:○	C:☐ F:○
3 ⇩ |a:	t: |s: |d:	t: |s: |d:	t: |s: |d:
	C:☐ F:○	C:☐ F:○	C:☐ F:○
4 ⇩ |a:	t: |s: |d:	t: |s: |d:	t: |s: |d:
	C:☐ F:○	C:☐ F:○	C:☐ F:○

Movement	Bunkai 1	Bunkai 2	Bunkai 3
5 ⇓ |a:	t: |s: |d: C:☐ F:◯	t: |s: |d: C:☐ F:◯	t: |s: |d: C:☐ F:◯
6 ⇨ |a:	t: |s: |d: C:☐ F:◯	t: |s: |d: C:☐ F:◯	t: |s: |d: C:☐ F:◯
7 ⇨ |a:	t: |s: |d: C:☐ F:◯	t: |s: |d: C:☐ F:◯	t: |s: |d: C:☐ F:◯
8 ⇓ |a:	t: |s: |d: C:☐ F:◯	t: |s: |d: C:☐ F:◯	t: |s: |d: C:☐ F:◯

Movement	Bunkai 1	Bunkai 2	Bunkai 3
9 ⇩ |a:	t: |s: |d: C:☐ F:○	t: |s: |d: C:☐ F:○	t: |s: |d: C:☐ F:○
10 ⇐ |a:	t: |s: |d: C:☐ F:○	t: |s: |d: C:☐ F:○	t: |s: |d: C:☐ F:○
11 ⇐ |a:	t: |s: |d: C:☐ F:○	t: |s: |d: C:☐ F:○	t: |s: |d: C:☐ F:○
12 ⇐ |a:	t: |s: |d: C:☐ F:○	t: |s: |d: C:☐ F:○	t: |s: |d: C:☐ F:○

Movement	Bunkai 1	Bunkai 2	Bunkai 3
13 ⇐ |a:	t: |s: |d: C:☐ F:◯	t: |s: |d: C:☐ F:◯	t: |s: |d: C:☐ F:◯
14 ⇓ |a:	t: |s: |d: C:☐ F:◯	t: |s: |d: C:☐ F:◯	t: |s: |d: C:☐ F:◯
15 ⇓ |a:	t: |s: |d: C:☐ F:◯	t: |s: |d: C:☐ F:◯	t: |s: |d: C:☐ F:◯
16 ⇓ |a:	t: |s: |d: C:☐ F:◯	t: |s: |d: C:☐ F:◯	t: |s: |d: C:☐ F:◯

Movement	Bunkai 1	Bunkai 2	Bunkai 3
17 ⇩ |a:	t: |s: |d: C:☐ F:○	t: |s: |d: C:☐ F:○	t: |s: |d: C:☐ F:○
18 ⇐ |a:	t: |s: |d: C:☐ F:○	t: |s: |d: C:☐ F:○	t: |s: |d: C:☐ F:○
19 ⇐ |a:	t: |s: |d: C:☐ F:○	t: |s: |d: C:☐ F:○	t: |s: |d: C:☐ F:○
20 ⇨ |a:	t: |s: |d: C:☐ F:○	t: |s: |d: C:☐ F:○	t: |s: |d: C:☐ F:○

Movement	Bunkai 1	Bunkai 2	Bunkai 3
21 ⇨ |a:	t: |s: |d: C:☐ F:◯	t: |s: |d: C:☐ F:◯	t: |s: |d: C:☐ F:◯
22 ⇦ |a:	t: |s: |d: C:☐ F:◯	t: |s: |d: C:☐ F:◯	t: |s: |d: C:☐ F:◯
23 ⇦ |a:	t: |s: |d: C:☐ F:◯	t: |s: |d: C:☐ F:◯	t: |s: |d: C:☐ F:◯
24 ⇦ |a:	t: |s: |d: C:☐ F:◯	t: |s: |d: C:☐ F:◯	t: |s: |d: C:☐ F:◯

Bunkai Notebook - Isshinryu

Movement	Bunkai 1	Bunkai 2	Bunkai 3
25 ⇐ |a:	t: |s: |d:	t: |s: |d:	t: |s: |d:
	C:☐ F:○	C:☐ F:○	C:☐ F:○
26 ⇐ |a:	t: |s: |d:	t: |s: |d:	t: |s: |d:
	C:☐ F:○	C:☐ F:○	C:☐ F:○
27 ⇩ |a:	t: |s: |d:	t: |s: |d:	t: |s: |d:
	C:☐ F:○	C:☐ F:○	C:☐ F:○
28 ⇨ |a:	t: |s: |d:	t: |s: |d:	t: |s: |d:
	C:☐ F:○	C:☐ F:○	C:☐ F:○

Movement	Bunkai 1	Bunkai 2	Bunkai 3
29 ⇨ |a:	t: |s: |d: c:☐ f:○	t: |s: |d: c:☐ f:○	t: |s: |d: c:☐ f:○
30 ⇨ |a:	t: |s: |d: c:☐ f:○	t: |s: |d: c:☐ f:○	t: |s: |d: c:☐ f:○
31 ⇨ |a:	t: |s: |d: c:☐ f:○	t: |s: |d: c:☐ f:○	t: |s: |d: c:☐ f:○
32 ⇨ |a:	t: |s: |d: c:☐ f:○	t: |s: |d: c:☐ f:○	t: |s: |d: c:☐ f:○

Movement	Bunkai 1	Bunkai 2	Bunkai 3
33 ⇩ |a:	t: |s: |d: C:☐ F:◯	t: |s: |d: C:☐ F:◯	t: |s: |d: C:☐ F:◯
34 ⇩ |a:	t: |s: |d: C:☐ F:◯	t: |s: |d: C:☐ F:◯	t: |s: |d: C:☐ F:◯
35 ⇩ |a:	t: |s: |d: C:☐ F:◯	t: |s: |d: C:☐ F:◯	t: |s: |d: C:☐ F:◯
36 ⇩ |a:	t: |s: |d: C:☐ F:◯	t: |s: |d: C:☐ F:◯	t: |s: |d: C:☐ F:◯

Movement	Bunkai 1	Bunkai 2	Bunkai 3
37 ⇨ |a:	t: |s: |d: C:☐ F:◯	t: |s: |d: C:☐ F:◯	t: |s: |d: C:☐ F:◯
38 ⇨ |a:	t: |s: |d: C:☐ F:◯	t: |s: |d: C:☐ F:◯	t: |s: |d: C:☐ F:◯
39 ⇐ |a:	t: |s: |d: C:☐ F:◯	t: |s: |d: C:☐ F:◯	t: |s: |d: C:☐ F:◯
40 ⇐ |a:	t: |s: |d: C:☐ F:◯	t: |s: |d: C:☐ F:◯	t: |s: |d: C:☐ F:◯

Movement	Bunkai 1	Bunkai 2	Bunkai 3
41 ⇨ |a:	t: |s: |d:	t: |s: |d:	t: |s: |d:
	C:☐ F:◯	C:☐ F:◯	C:☐ F:◯
42 ⇨ |a:	t: |s: |d:	t: |s: |d:	t: |s: |d:
	C:☐ F:◯	C:☐ F:◯	C:☐ F:◯
43 ⇨ |a:	t: |s: |d:	t: |s: |d:	t: |s: |d:
	C:☐ F:◯	C:☐ F:◯	C:☐ F:◯
44 ⇩ |a:	t: |s: |d:	t: |s: |d:	t: |s: |d:
	C:☐ F:◯	C:☐ F:◯	C:☐ F:◯

Movement	Bunkai 1	Bunkai 2	Bunkai 3
45 ⇩ |a:	t: |s: |d:	t: |s: |d:	t: |s: |d:
	C:☐ F:◯	C:☐ F:◯	C:☐ F:◯
46 ⇩ |a:	t: |s: |d:	t: |s: |d:	t: |s: |d:
	C:☐ F:◯	C:☐ F:◯	C:☐ F:◯
47 ⇩ |a:	t: |s: |d:	t: |s: |d:	t: |s: |d:
	C:☐ F:◯	C:☐ F:◯	C:☐ F:◯

Naihanchi Breakdown

This section gives a brief explanation of each movement, following the numbering of the photos. Reminder - this is provided for reference only (see Note on page 8).

1. Stand at attention
2. Bow
3. Salutation
4. Turn feet into Naihanchi stance
5. Cross right foot over left
6. Step out with left foot, inverted ridgehand
7. Right arm elbow strike into left hand
8. Stack hands on left hip
9. Draw up right foot
10. Right hand leg block to right side
11. Gouge right with left hand
12. Step across with left foot
13. Draw up right foot
14. Left hand inverted ridgehand
15. Left hand hammer strike
16. Right hand upward elbow strike
17. Right hand backfist
18. Draw up right foot
19. Right hand backfist to right
20. Draw up left foot
21. Right hand hammerfist to left
22. Stack hands on left hip, right foot up
23. Both hands on hips preparing for...
24. Double punch to the right
25. Right hand inverted rigehand to right
26. Left elbow strike into right hand
27. Stack hands on right hip

28. Draw up left foot
29. Left hand leg block to left
30. Right hand gouge across to left
31. Step across with right foot
32. Draw left foot up
33. Right hand inverted ridgehand to front
34. Right hand downward hammerfist
35. Left upwards elbow strike
36. Left outward backfist
37. Draw up left foot
38. Left hand backfist to left
39. Draw up right foot
40. Left hand hammerfist to right
41. Stack hands on right hip, draw up left foot
42. Both hands on hips preparing for...
43. Double punch to left
44. Draw feet together to stand at attention
45. Closing salutation
46. Bow
47. End of kata

Wansu
Kata

Note: Photos were taken at an angle that shows each movement best – refer to arrows for direction faced in that particular movement. See "Note" on page 8.

Movement	Bunkai 1	Bunkai 2	Bunkai 3
1 ⇩ |a:	t: |s: |d: C:☐ F:◯	t: |s: |d: C:☐ F:◯	t: |s: |d: C:☐ F:◯
2 ⇩ |a:	t: |s: |d: C:☐ F:◯	t: |s: |d: C:☐ F:◯	t: |s: |d: C:☐ F:◯
3 ⇩ |a:	t: |s: |d: C:☐ F:◯	t: |s: |d: C:☐ F:◯	t: |s: |d: C:☐ F:◯
4 ⇩ |a:	t: |s: |d: C:☐ F:◯	t: |s: |d: C:☐ F:◯	t: |s: |d: C:☐ F:◯

Movement	Bunkai 1	Bunkai 2	Bunkai 3
5 ⇨ |a:	t: |s: |d: C:☐ F:◯	t: |s: |d: C:☐ F:◯	t: |s: |d: C:☐ F:◯
6 ⇨ |a:	t: |s: |d: C:☐ F:◯	t: |s: |d: C:☐ F:◯	t: |s: |d: C:☐ F:◯
7 ⇩ |a:	t: |s: |d: C:☐ F:◯	t: |s: |d: C:☐ F:◯	t: |s: |d: C:☐ F:◯
8 ⇩ |a:	t: |s: |d: C:☐ F:◯	t: |s: |d: C:☐ F:◯	t: |s: |d: C:☐ F:◯

Movement	Bunkai 1	Bunkai 2	Bunkai 3
9 ⇩ |a:	t: |s: |d: C:☐F:○	t: |s: |d: C:☐F:○	t: |s: |d: C:☐F:○
10 ⇩ |a:	t: |s: |d: C:☐F:○	t: |s: |d: C:☐F:○	t: |s: |d: C:☐F:○
11 ⇩ |a:	t: |s: |d: C:☐F:○	t: |s: |d: C:☐F:○	t: |s: |d: C:☐F:○
12 ⇩ |a:	t: |s: |d: C:☐F:○	t: |s: |d: C:☐F:○	t: |s: |d: C:☐F:○

Movement	Bunkai 1	Bunkai 2	Bunkai 3
13 ⇧ |a:	t: |s: |d:	t: |s: |d:	t: |s: |d:
	C:☐ F:◯	C:☐ F:◯	C:☐ F:◯
14 ⇧ |a:	t: |s: |d:	t: |s: |d:	t: |s: |d:
	C:☐ F:◯	C:☐ F:◯	C:☐ F:◯
15 ⇧ |a:	t: |s: |d:	t: |s: |d:	t: |s: |d:
	C:☐ F:◯	C:☐ F:◯	C:☐ F:◯
16 ⇧ |a:	t: |s: |d:	t: |s: |d:	t: |s: |d:
	C:☐ F:◯	C:☐ F:◯	C:☐ F:◯

Movement	Bunkai 1	Bunkai 2	Bunkai 3
17 ⇧ |a:	t: |s: |d: C:☐ F:◯	t: |s: |d: C:☐ F:◯	t: |s: |d: C:☐ F:◯
18 ⇧ |a:	t: |s: |d: C:☐ F:◯	t: |s: |d: C:☐ F:◯	t: |s: |d: C:☐ F:◯
19 ⇩ |a:	t: |s: |d: C:☐ F:◯	t: |s: |d: C:☐ F:◯	t: |s: |d: C:☐ F:◯
20 ⇩ |a:	t: |s: |d: C:☐ F:◯	t: |s: |d: C:☐ F:◯	t: |s: |d: C:☐ F:◯

Movement	Bunkai 1	Bunkai 2	Bunkai 3
21 ⇩ |a:	t: |s: |d: C:☐ F:◯	t: |s: |d: C:☐ F:◯	t: |s: |d: C:☐ F:◯
22 ⇩ |a:	t: |s: |d: C:☐ F:◯	t: |s: |d: C:☐ F:◯	t: |s: |d: C:☐ F:◯
23 ⇩ |a:	t: |s: |d: C:☐ F:◯	t: |s: |d: C:☐ F:◯	t: |s: |d: C:☐ F:◯
24 ⇩ |a:	t: |s: |d: C:☐ F:◯	t: |s: |d: C:☐ F:◯	t: |s: |d: C:☐ F:◯

Movement	Bunkai 1	Bunkai 2	Bunkai 3
25 ⇐ |a:	t: |s: |d: C:☐F:○	t: |s: |d: C:☐F:○	t: |s: |d: C:☐F:○
26 ⇨ |a:	t: |s: |d: C:☐F:○	t: |s: |d: C:☐F:○	t: |s: |d: C:☐F:○
27 ⇨ |a:	t: |s: |d: C:☐F:○	t: |s: |d: C:☐F:○	t: |s: |d: C:☐F:○
28 ⇨ |a:	t: |s: |d: C:☐F:○	t: |s: |d: C:☐F:○	t: |s: |d: C:☐F:○

Movement	Bunkai 1	Bunkai 2	Bunkai 3
29 ⇩ a:	t: s: d:	t: s: d:	t: s: d:
	C:☐ F:○	C:☐ F:○	C:☐ F:○
30 ⇦ a:	t: s: d:	t: s: d:	t: s: d:
	C:☐ F:○	C:☐ F:○	C:☐ F:○
31 ⇦ a:	t: s: d:	t: s: d:	t: s: d:
	C:☐ F:○	C:☐ F:○	C:☐ F:○
32 ⇦ a:	t: s: d:	t: s: d:	t: s: d:
	C:☐ F:○	C:☐ F:○	C:☐ F:○

Movement	Bunkai 1	Bunkai 2	Bunkai 3
33 ⇩ |a:	t: |s: |d: C:☐ F:◯	t: |s: |d: C:☐ F:◯	t: |s: |d: C:☐ F:◯
34 ⇩ |a:	t: |s: |d: C:☐ F:◯	t: |s: |d: C:☐ F:◯	t: |s: |d: C:☐ F:◯
35 ⇩ |a:	t: |s: |d: C:☐ F:◯	t: |s: |d: C:☐ F:◯	t: |s: |d: C:☐ F:◯
36 ⇩ |a:	t: |s: |d: C:☐ F:◯	t: |s: |d: C:☐ F:◯	t: |s: |d: C:☐ F:◯

Movement	Bunkai 1	Bunkai 2	Bunkai 3
37 ⇩ |a:	t: |s: |d: C:☐ F:○	t: |s: |d: C:☐ F:○	t: |s: |d: C:☐ F:○
38 ⇩ |a:	t: |s: |d: C:☐ F:○	t: |s: |d: C:☐ F:○	t: |s: |d: C:☐ F:○
39 ⇩ |a:	t: |s: |d: C:☐ F:○	t: |s: |d: C:☐ F:○	t: |s: |d: C:☐ F:○
40 ⇨ |a:	t: |s: |d: C:☐ F:○	t: |s: |d: C:☐ F:○	t: |s: |d: C:☐ F:○

Movement	Bunkai 1	Bunkai 2	Bunkai 3
41 ⇩ |a:	t: |s: |d: c:☐ f:◯	t: |s: |d: c:☐ f:◯	t: |s: |d: c:☐ f:◯
42 ⇐ |a:	t: |s: |d: c:☐ f:◯	t: |s: |d: c:☐ f:◯	t: |s: |d: c:☐ f:◯
43 ⇩ |a:	t: |s: |d: c:☐ f:◯	t: |s: |d: c:☐ f:◯	t: |s: |d: c:☐ f:◯
44 ⇩ |a:	t: |s: |d: c:☐ f:◯	t: |s: |d: c:☐ f:◯	t: |s: |d: c:☐ f:◯

Movement	Bunkai 1	Bunkai 2	Bunkai 3
45 ⇧ |a:	t: |s: |d: C:☐ F:◯	t: |s: |d: C:☐ F:◯	t: |s: |d: C:☐ F:◯
46 ⇧ |a:	t: |s: |d: C:☐ F:◯	t: |s: |d: C:☐ F:◯	t: |s: |d: C:☐ F:◯
47 ⇩ |a:	t: |s: |d: C:☐ F:◯	t: |s: |d: C:☐ F:◯	t: |s: |d: C:☐ F:◯
48 ⇩ |a:	t: |s: |d: C:☐ F:◯	t: |s: |d: C:☐ F:◯	t: |s: |d: C:☐ F:◯

Movement	Bunkai 1	Bunkai 2	Bunkai 3
49 ⇩ |a:	t: |s: |d: C:☐ F:○	t: |s: |d: C:☐ F:○	t: |s: |d: C:☐ F:○
50 ⇩ |a:	t: |s: |d: C:☐ F:○	t: |s: |d: C:☐ F:○	t: |s: |d: C:☐ F:○
51 ⇩ |a:	t: |s: |d: C:☐ F:○	t: |s: |d: C:☐ F:○	t: |s: |d: C:☐ F:○
52 ⇩ |a:	t: |s: |d: C:☐ F:○	t: |s: |d: C:☐ F:○	t: |s: |d: C:☐ F:○

Movement	Bunkai 1	Bunkai 2	Bunkai 3
53 ⇩ |a:	t: |s: |d:	t: |s: |d:	t: |s: |d:
	c:☐ f:◯	c:☐ f:◯	c:☐ f:◯
54 ⇩ |a:	t: |s: |d:	t: |s: |d:	t: |s: |d:
	c:☐ f:◯	c:☐ f:◯	c:☐ f:◯
55 ⇩ |a:	t: |s: |d:	t: |s: |d:	t: |s: |d:
	c:☐ f:◯	c:☐ f:◯	c:☐ f:◯

Wansu Breakdown

This section gives a brief explanation of each movement, following the numbering of the photos. Reminder - this is provided for reference only (see Note on page 8).

1. Stand at attention
2. Bow
3. Salutation
4. Step out with right foot, left hand over right fist
5. Left hand leg block to left
6. Right hand punch to left
7. Step up with left foot, left hand leg block
8. Right hand punch
9. Step up with right foot, right hand open arc sweep
10. Gouge with left hand, right hand guard
11. Step behind with left foot, close left hand
12. Right hand punch
13. Pivot 180°, left hand leg block
14. Right hand punch
15. Step up with right foot, right hand open arc sweep
16. Gouge with left hand, right hand guard
17. Step behind with left foot, close left hand
18. Right hand punch
19. Pivot 180°, left hand open arc sweep
20. Reinforced right punch, left hand supporting
21. Right foot straight kick
22. Set down in Seiunchin stance, left hand at forehead, right hand low
23. Draw back with right foot, open both hands
24. Set back into Seiunchin stance, close both hands
25. Pivot on left foot 270°, right hand push down
26. Pivot 180°, left hand chop

27. Right knee strike
28. Right hand punch
29. Pivot 90°, look to right
30. Pivot 90°, right hand chop
31. Left knee strike
32. Left hand punch
33. Pivot 90° to the left and draw feet together
34. Step out with right foot, left hand punch on 45°
35. Right hand punch on 45°
36. Draw back foot up
37. Step out with left foot, right hand punch on 45°
38. Left hand punch on 45°
39. Draw feet together, stack hands on right hip
40. Left foot side kick
41. Stack hands on left hip
42. Right foot side kick
43. Left foot forward guard position
44. Step up with right foot, right elbow strike
45. Draw back 180°, check with left knee
46. Left foot straight kick
47. Draw back 180°, check with right knee
48. Right foot straight kick
49. Set down in right foot forward Seisan stance...
50. Double hand chop outwards
51. Left hand to belt, right hand guard
52. Bring feet together
53. Closing salutation
54. Bow
55. End of kata

Chinto
Kata

Note: Photos were taken at an angle that shows each movement best – refer to arrows for direction faced in that particular movement. See "Note" on page 8.

Movement	Bunkai 1	Bunkai 2	Bunkai 3
1 ⇩ |a:	t: |s: |d: C:☐ F:○	t: |s: |d: C:☐ F:○	t: |s: |d: C:☐ F:○
2 ⇩ |a:	t: |s: |d: C:☐ F:○	t: |s: |d: C:☐ F:○	t: |s: |d: C:☐ F:○
3 ⇩ |a:	t: |s: |d: C:☐ F:○	t: |s: |d: C:☐ F:○	t: |s: |d: C:☐ F:○
4 ⇩ |a:	t: |s: |d: C:☐ F:○	t: |s: |d: C:☐ F:○	t: |s: |d: C:☐ F:○

Movement	Bunkai 1	Bunkai 2	Bunkai 3
5 ↘ |a:	t: |s: |d: C:☐ F:◯	t: |s: |d: C:☐ F:◯	t: |s: |d: C:☐ F:◯
6 ↘ |a:	t: |s: |d: C:☐ F:◯	t: |s: |d: C:☐ F:◯	t: |s: |d: C:☐ F:◯
7 ↘ |a:	t: |s: |d: C:☐ F:◯	t: |s: |d: C:☐ F:◯	t: |s: |d: C:☐ F:◯
8 ↘ |a:	t: |s: |d: C:☐ F:◯	t: |s: |d: C:☐ F:◯	t: |s: |d: C:☐ F:◯

Movement	Bunkai 1	Bunkai 2	Bunkai 3
9 ↘ |a:	t: |s: |d:	t: |s: |d:	t: |s: |d:
	C:☐ F:○	C:☐ F:○	C:☐ F:○
10 ↘ |a:	t: |s: |d:	t: |s: |d:	t: |s: |d:
	C:☐ F:○	C:☐ F:○	C:☐ F:○
11 ↘ |a:	t: |s: |d:	t: |s: |d:	t: |s: |d:
	C:☐ F:○	C:☐ F:○	C:☐ F:○
12 ↘ |a:	t: |s: |d:	t: |s: |d:	t: |s: |d:
	C:☐ F:○	C:☐ F:○	C:☐ F:○

Movement	Bunkai 1	Bunkai 2	Bunkai 3
13 ⤸ |a:	t: |s: |d: C:☐ F:◯	t: |s: |d: C:☐ F:◯	t: |s: |d: C:☐ F:◯
14 ⤸ |a:	t: |s: |d: C:☐ F:◯	t: |s: |d: C:☐ F:◯	t: |s: |d: C:☐ F:◯
15 ⬀ |a:	t: |s: |d: C:☐ F:◯	t: |s: |d: C:☐ F:◯	t: |s: |d: C:☐ F:◯
16 ⤸ |a:	t: |s: |d: C:☐ F:◯	t: |s: |d: C:☐ F:◯	t: |s: |d: C:☐ F:◯

Movement	Bunkai 1	Bunkai 2	Bunkai 3
17 ↘ |a:	t: |s: |d: c:☐F:○	t: |s: |d: c:☐F:○	t: |s: |d: c:☐F:○
18 ↘ |a:	t: |s: |d: c:☐F:○	t: |s: |d: c:☐F:○	t: |s: |d: c:☐F:○
19 ↘ |a:	t: |s: |d: c:☐F:○	t: |s: |d: c:☐F:○	t: |s: |d: c:☐F:○
20 ↘ |a:	t: |s: |d: c:☐F:○	t: |s: |d: c:☐F:○	t: |s: |d: c:☐F:○

Movement	Bunkai 1	Bunkai 2	Bunkai 3
21 ↘ |a:	t: |s: |d: c:☐ f:○	t: |s: |d: c:☐ f:○	t: |s: |d: c:☐ f:○
22 ↘ |a:	t: |s: |d: c:☐ f:○	t: |s: |d: c:☐ f:○	t: |s: |d: c:☐ f:○
23 ↘ |a:	t: |s: |d: c:☐ f:○	t: |s: |d: c:☐ f:○	t: |s: |d: c:☐ f:○
24 ↗ |a:	t: |s: |d: c:☐ f:○	t: |s: |d: c:☐ f:○	t: |s: |d: c:☐ f:○

Movement	Bunkai 1	Bunkai 2	Bunkai 3
25 ↘ |a:	t: |s: |d: C:☐ F:◯	t: |s: |d: C:☐ F:◯	t: |s: |d: C:☐ F:◯
26 ↘ |a:	t: |s: |d: C:☐ F:◯	t: |s: |d: C:☐ F:◯	t: |s: |d: C:☐ F:◯
27 ↘ |a:	t: |s: |d: C:☐ F:◯	t: |s: |d: C:☐ F:◯	t: |s: |d: C:☐ F:◯
28 ↘ |a:	t: |s: |d: C:☐ F:◯	t: |s: |d: C:☐ F:◯	t: |s: |d: C:☐ F:◯

Movement	Bunkai 1	Bunkai 2	Bunkai 3
29 ↖ |a:	t: |s: |d: C:☐ F:◯	t: |s: |d: C:☐ F:◯	t: |s: |d: C:☐ F:◯
30 ↖ |a:	t: |s: |d: C:☐ F:◯	t: |s: |d: C:☐ F:◯	t: |s: |d: C:☐ F:◯
31 ↖ |a:	t: |s: |d: C:☐ F:◯	t: |s: |d: C:☐ F:◯	t: |s: |d: C:☐ F:◯
32 ↗ |a:	t: |s: |d: C:☐ F:◯	t: |s: |d: C:☐ F:◯	t: |s: |d: C:☐ F:◯

97

Movement	Bunkai 1	Bunkai 2	Bunkai 3
33 ↙ |a:	t: |s: |d: c:☐ F:○	t: |s: |d: c:☐ F:○	t: |s: |d: c:☐ F:○
34 ↘ |a:	t: |s: |d: c:☐ F:○	t: |s: |d: c:☐ F:○	t: |s: |d: c:☐ F:○
35 ↘ |a:	t: |s: |d: c:☐ F:○	t: |s: |d: c:☐ F:○	t: |s: |d: c:☐ F:○
36 ↘ |a:	t: |s: |d: c:☐ F:○	t: |s: |d: c:☐ F:○	t: |s: |d: c:☐ F:○

Movement	Bunkai 1	Bunkai 2	Bunkai 3
37 ↘ |a:	t: |s: |d: C:☐ F:○	t: |s: |d: C:☐ F:○	t: |s: |d: C:☐ F:○
38 ↙ |a:	t: |s: |d: C:☐ F:○	t: |s: |d: C:☐ F:○	t: |s: |d: C:☐ F:○
39 ↙ |a:	t: |s: |d: C:☐ F:○	t: |s: |d: C:☐ F:○	t: |s: |d: C:☐ F:○
40 ↗ |a:	t: |s: |d: C:☐ F:○	t: |s: |d: C:☐ F:○	t: |s: |d: C:☐ F:○

Movement	Bunkai 1	Bunkai 2	Bunkai 3
41 ⇘ |a:	t: |s: |d: C:☐ F:○	t: |s: |d: C:☐ F:○	t: |s: |d: C:☐ F:○
42 ⇘ |a:	t: |s: |d: C:☐ F:○	t: |s: |d: C:☐ F:○	t: |s: |d: C:☐ F:○
43 ⇘ |a:	t: |s: |d: C:☐ F:○	t: |s: |d: C:☐ F:○	t: |s: |d: C:☐ F:○
44 ⇘ |a:	t: |s: |d: C:☐ F:○	t: |s: |d: C:☐ F:○	t: |s: |d: C:☐ F:○

Movement	Bunkai 1	Bunkai 2	Bunkai 3
45 ⤴ |a:	t: |s: |d: C:☐ F:◯	t: |s: |d: C:☐ F:◯	t: |s: |d: C:☐ F:◯
46 ⤵ |a:	t: |s: |d: C:☐ F:◯	t: |s: |d: C:☐ F:◯	t: |s: |d: C:☐ F:◯
47 ⤵ |a:	t: |s: |d: C:☐ F:◯	t: |s: |d: C:☐ F:◯	t: |s: |d: C:☐ F:◯
48 ⤵ |a:	t: |s: |d: C:☐ F:◯	t: |s: |d: C:☐ F:◯	t: |s: |d: C:☐ F:◯

Movement	Bunkai 1	Bunkai 2	Bunkai 3
49 ↘ |a:	t: |s: |d: C:☐F:◯	t: |s: |d: C:☐F:◯	t: |s: |d: C:☐F:◯
50 ↘ |a:	t: |s: |d: C:☐F:◯	t: |s: |d: C:☐F:◯	t: |s: |d: C:☐F:◯
51 ↘ |a:	t: |s: |d: C:☐F:◯	t: |s: |d: C:☐F:◯	t: |s: |d: C:☐F:◯
52 ↘ |a:	t: |s: |d: C:☐F:◯	t: |s: |d: C:☐F:◯	t: |s: |d: C:☐F:◯

Movement	Bunkai 1	Bunkai 2	Bunkai 3
53 ↖ |a:	t: |s: |d: C:☐ F:◯	t: |s: |d: C:☐ F:◯	t: |s: |d: C:☐ F:◯
54 ↖ |a:	t: |s: |d: C:☐ F:◯	t: |s: |d: C:☐ F:◯	t: |s: |d: C:☐ F:◯
55 ↖ |a:	t: |s: |d: C:☐ F:◯	t: |s: |d: C:☐ F:◯	t: |s: |d: C:☐ F:◯
56 ↖ |a:	t: |s: |d: C:☐ F:◯	t: |s: |d: C:☐ F:◯	t: |s: |d: C:☐ F:◯

Movement	Bunkai 1	Bunkai 2	Bunkai 3
57 ↖ |a:	t: |s: |d:	t: |s: |d:	t: |s: |d:
	C:☐ F:◯	C:☐ F:◯	C:☐ F:◯
58 ⇓ |a:	t: |s: |d:	t: |s: |d:	t: |s: |d:
	C:☐ F:◯	C:☐ F:◯	C:☐ F:◯
59 ⇓ |a:	t: |s: |d:	t: |s: |d:	t: |s: |d:
	C:☐ F:◯	C:☐ F:◯	C:☐ F:◯
60 ⇓ |a:	t: |s: |d:	t: |s: |d:	t: |s: |d:
	C:☐ F:◯	C:☐ F:◯	C:☐ F:◯

Chinto Breakdown

This section gives a brief explanation of each movement, following the numbering of the photos. Reminder - this is provided for reference only (see Note on page 8).

1. Stand at attention
2. Bow
3. Salutation
4. Ready stance
5. Step back on 45° in cat stance, x-block
6. Gouge with right hand underneath left hand
7. Backfist with left hand
8. Shuffle up, punch with right hand
9. Shuffle up, squat block
10. Pivot 360°on right foot, left hand leg block
11. Draw back into cat stance, x-block
12. Double-jump kick, first part (right leg)
13. Double-jump kick, second part (left leg)
14. Downward x-block
15. Pivot 180°, downward x-block
16. Look 180°, punch with right hand
17. Step up with left foot, left hand punch
18. Right elbow strike into left hand
19. Guard position
20. Pivot back foot into Seiunchin stance, draw hands back
21. Step up 180°
22. Double-hand strike
23. Double-hand chop down
24. Pivot back foot into Seiunchin stance, double punch down
25. Pivot into Seisan stance, right hand open arc sweep
26. Left forearm smash into right hand

27. Step back with right foot, left hand over right fist
28. Downward push block
29. Step back into crane stance with left foot
30. Double down block
31. Stack hands on hips, right straight kick
32. Set foot down in Seiunchin stance, prepare for…
33. Double punch down
34. Pivot into crane stance, break upward
35. Step up left foot, left hand leg block right hand head block
36. Step up right foot, right hand leg block left hand head block
37. Pivot 360°, left hand leg block
38. Turn 180°, double break up
39. Step up with right foot, right elbow strike
40. Double punch down
41. Pivot into crane stance, double break up
42. Left straight kick, set down in left foot forward Seisan stance
43. Step up with right foot
44. Right hand straight punch
45. Double punch in
46. Step back with right foot into crane
47. Double down block
48. Right foot kick
49. Step back 180° with right foot into crane stance
50. Double down block
51. Hands on hips, straighten foot
52. Left straight kick
53. Keep leg up, left hand…
54. Open arc sweep
55. Right forearm smash into left hand
56. Right straight kick

57. Left hand punch while on left knee
58. Draw back up to ready stance
59. Closing salutation
60. Bow

Kusanku
Kata

Note: Photos were taken at an angle that shows each movement best – refer to arrows for direction faced in that particular movement. See "Note" on page 8.

Movement	Bunkai 1	Bunkai 2	Bunkai 3
1 ⇩ |a:	t: |s: |d: C:☐F:○	t: |s: |d: C:☐F:○	t: |s: |d: C:☐F:○
2 ⇩ |a:	t: |s: |d: C:☐F:○	t: |s: |d: C:☐F:○	t: |s: |d: C:☐F:○
3 ⇩ |a:	t: |s: |d: C:☐F:○	t: |s: |d: C:☐F:○	t: |s: |d: C:☐F:○
4 ⇩ |a:	t: |s: |d: C:☐F:○	t: |s: |d: C:☐F:○	t: |s: |d: C:☐F:○

Movement	Bunkai 1	Bunkai 2	Bunkai 3
5⇩ |a:	t: |s: |d:	t: |s: |d:	t: |s: |d:
	C:☐ F:○	C:☐ F:○	C:☐ F:○
6⇩ |a:	t: |s: |d:	t: |s: |d:	t: |s: |d:
	C:☐ F:○	C:☐ F:○	C:☐ F:○
7⇩ |a:	t: |s: |d:	t: |s: |d:	t: |s: |d:
	C:☐ F:○	C:☐ F:○	C:☐ F:○
8⇩ |a:	t: |s: |d:	t: |s: |d:	t: |s: |d:
	C:☐ F:○	C:☐ F:○	C:☐ F:○

Movement	Bunkai 1	Bunkai 2	Bunkai 3
9⇩ |a:	t: |s: |d: C:☐ F:◯	t: |s: |d: C:☐ F:◯	t: |s: |d: C:☐ F:◯
10⇩ |a:	t: |s: |d: C:☐ F:◯	t: |s: |d: C:☐ F:◯	t: |s: |d: C:☐ F:◯
11⇩ |a:	t: |s: |d: C:☐ F:◯	t: |s: |d: C:☐ F:◯	t: |s: |d: C:☐ F:◯
12⇩ |a:	t: |s: |d: C:☐ F:◯	t: |s: |d: C:☐ F:◯	t: |s: |d: C:☐ F:◯

Movement	Bunkai 1	Bunkai 2	Bunkai 3
13⇩ |a:	t: |s: |d: C:☐ F:◯	t: |s: |d: C:☐ F:◯	t: |s: |d: C:☐ F:◯
14⇩ |a:	t: |s: |d: C:☐ F:◯	t: |s: |d: C:☐ F:◯	t: |s: |d: C:☐ F:◯
15⇩ |a:	t: |s: |d: C:☐ F:◯	t: |s: |d: C:☐ F:◯	t: |s: |d: C:☐ F:◯
16⇩ |a:	t: |s: |d: C:☐ F:◯	t: |s: |d: C:☐ F:◯	t: |s: |d: C:☐ F:◯

Movement	Bunkai 1	Bunkai 2	Bunkai 3
17⇩ | a:	t: | s: | d: C:☐ F:◯	t: | s: | d: C:☐ F:◯	t: | s: | d: C:☐ F:◯
18⇩ | a:	t: | s: | d: C:☐ F:◯	t: | s: | d: C:☐ F:◯	t: | s: | d: C:☐ F:◯
19⇧ | a:	t: | s: | d: C:☐ F:◯	t: | s: | d: C:☐ F:◯	t: | s: | d: C:☐ F:◯
20⇧ | a:	t: | s: | d: C:☐ F:◯	t: | s: | d: C:☐ F:◯	t: | s: | d: C:☐ F:◯

Movement	Bunkai 1	Bunkai 2	Bunkai 3
21 ⇩ | a:	t:　|s:　|d:　　　C:☐ F:○	t:　|s:　|d:　　　C:☐ F:○	t:　|s:　|d:　　　C:☐ F:○
22⇩ | a:	t:　|s:　|d:　　　C:☐ F:○	t:　|s:　|d:　　　C:☐ F:○	t:　|s:　|d:　　　C:☐ F:○
23⇩ | a:	t:　|s:　|d:　　　C:☐ F:○	t:　|s:　|d:　　　C:☐ F:○	t:　|s:　|d:　　　C:☐ F:○
24⇩ | a:	t:　|s:　|d:　　　C:☐ F:○	t:　|s:　|d:　　　C:☐ F:○	t:　|s:.　|d:　　　C:☐ F:○

Movement	Bunkai 1	Bunkai 2	Bunkai 3
25⇩ |a:	t:　|s:　|d: C:☐F:◯	t:　|s:　|d: C:☐F:◯	t:　|s:　|d: C:☐F:◯
26⇧ |a:	t:　|s:　|d: C:☐F:◯	t:　|s:　|d: C:☐F:◯	t:　|s:　|d: C:☐F:◯
27⇧ |a:	t:　|s:　|d: C:☐F:◯	t:　|s:　|d: C:☐F:◯	t:　|s:　|d: C:☐F:◯
28⇩ |a:	t:　|s:　|d: C:☐F:◯	t:　|s:　|d: C:☐F:◯	t:　|s:　|d: C:☐F:◯

Movement	Bunkai 1	Bunkai 2	Bunkai 3
29⇩ |a:	t: |s: |d: C:☐ F:○	t: |s: |d: C:☐ F:○	t: |s: |d: C:☐ F:○
30⇧ |a:	t: |s: |d: C:☐ F:○	t: |s: |d: C:☐ F:○	t: |s: |d: C:☐ F:○
31⇧ |a:	t: |s: |d: C:☐ F:○	t: |s: |d: C:☐ F:○	t: |s: |d: C:☐ F:○
32⇧ |a:	t: |s: |d: C:☐ F:○	t: |s: |d: C:☐ F:○	t: |s: |d: C:☐ F:○

Movement	Bunkai 1	Bunkai 2	Bunkai 3
33⇧ |a:	t: |s: |d: C:☐ F:◯	t: |s: |d: C:☐ F:◯	t: |s: |d: C:☐ F:◯
34⇩ |a:	t: |s: |d: C:☐ F:◯	t: |s: |d: C:☐ F:◯	t: |s: |d: C:☐ F:◯
35⇩ |a:	t: |s: |d: C:☐ F:◯	t: |s: |d: C:☐ F:◯	t: |s: |d: C:☐ F:◯
36⇨ |a:	t: |s: |d: C:☐ F:◯	t: |s: |d: C:☐ F:◯	t: |s: |d: C:☐ F:◯

Movement	Bunkai 1	Bunkai 2	Bunkai 3
37⇨ |a:	t: |s: |d: C:☐ F:〇	t: |s: |d: C:☐ F:〇	t: |s: |d: C:☐ F:〇
38⇨ |a:	t: |s: |d: C:☐ F:〇	t: |s: |d: C:☐ F:〇	t: |s: |d: C:☐ F:〇
39⇦ |a:	t: |s: |d: C:☐ F:〇	t: |s: |d: C:☐ F:〇	t: |s: |d: C:☐ F:〇
40⇦ |a:	t: |s: |d: C:☐ F:〇	t: |s: |d: C:☐ F:〇	t: |s: |d: C:☐ F:〇

Movement	Bunkai 1	Bunkai 2	Bunkai 3
41 ⇐ |a:	t: |s: |d: C:☐ F:○	t: |s: |d: C:☐ F:○	t: |s: |d: C:☐ F:○
42↘ |a:	t: |s: |d: C:☐ F:○	t: |s: |d: C:☐ F:○	t: |s: |d: C:☐ F:○
43↘ |a:	t: |s: |d: C:☐ F:○	t: |s: |d: C:☐ F:○	t: |s: |d: C:☐ F:○
44↙ |a:	t: |s: |d: C:☐ F:○	t: |s: |d: C:☐ F:○	t: |s: |d: C:☐ F:○

Movement	Bunkai 1	Bunkai 2	Bunkai 3
45↙ |a:	t: |s: |d: C:☐ F:○	t: |s: |d: C:☐ F:○	t: |s: |d: C:☐ F:○
46⇩ |a:	t: |s: |d: C:☐ F:○	t: |s: |d: C:☐ F:○	t: |s: |d: C:☐ F:○
47⇩ |a:	t: |s: |d: C:☐ F:○	t: |s: |d: C:☐ F:○	t: |s: |d: C:☐ F:○
48⇩ |a:	t: |s: |d: C:☐ F:○	t: |s: |d: C:☐ F:○	t: |s: |d: C:☐ F:○

Movement	Bunkai 1	Bunkai 2	Bunkai 3
49⇩ |a:	t: |s: |d: C:☐ F:◯	t: |s: |d: C:☐ F:◯	t: |s: |d: C:☐ F:◯
50⇩ |a:	t: |s: |d: C:☐ F:◯	t: |s: |d: C:☐ F:◯	t: |s: |d: C:☐ F:◯
51⇩ |a:	t: |s: |d: C:☐ F:◯	t: |s: |d: C:☐ F:◯	t: |s: |d: C:☐ F:◯
52⇩ |a:	t: |s: |d: C:☐ F:◯	t: |s: |d: C:☐ F:◯	t: |s: |d: C:☐ F:◯

Movement	Bunkai 1	Bunkai 2	Bunkai 3
53⇩ |a:	t: |s: |d: C:☐ F:○	t: |s: |d: C:☐ F:○	t: |s: |d: C:☐ F:○
54⇧ |a:	t: |s: |d: C:☐ F:○	t: |s: |d: C:☐ F:○	t: |s: |d: C:☐ F:○
55⇧ |a:	t: |s: |d: C:☐ F:○	t: |s: |d: C:☐ F:○	t: |s: |d: C:☐ F:○
56⇧ |a:	t: |s: |d: C:☐ F:○	t: |s: |d: C:☐ F:○	t: |s: |d: C:☐ F:○

Movement	Bunkai 1	Bunkai 2	Bunkai 3
57⇩ |a:	t: |s: |d: C:☐F:○	t: |s: |d: C:☐F:○	t: |s: |d: C:☐F:○
58⇧ |a:	t: |s: |d: C:☐F:○	t: |s: |d: C:☐F:○	t: |s: |d: C:☐F:○
59⇧|a:	t: |s: |d: C:☐F:○	t: |s: |d: C:☐F:○	t: |s: |d: C:☐F:○
60⇧ |a:	t: |s: |d: C:☐F:○	t: |s: |d: C:☐F:○	t: |s: |d: C:☐F:○

Movement	Bunkai 1	Bunkai 2	Bunkai 3
61 ⇧ |a:	t: |s: |d:	t: |s: |d:	t: |s: |d:
	C:☐ F:◯	C:☐ F:◯	C:☐ F:◯
62⇩ |a:	t: |s: |d:	t: |s: |d:	t: |s: |d:
	C:☐ F:◯	C:☐ F:◯	C:☐ F:◯
63⇩ |a:	t: |s: |d:	t: |s: |d:	t: |s: |d:
	C:☐ F:◯	C:☐ F:◯	C:☐ F:◯
64⇩ |a:	t: |s: |d:	t: |s: |d:	t: |s: |d:
	C:☐ F:◯	C:☐ F:◯	C:☐ F:◯

Movement	Bunkai 1	Bunkai 2	Bunkai 3
65↘ |a:	t: |s: |d: C:☐ F:○	t: |s: |d: C:☐ F:○	t: |s: |d: C:☐ F:○
66↘ |a:	t: |s: |d: C:☐ F:○	t: |s: |d: C:☐ F:○	t: |s: |d: C:☐ F:○
67↘ |a:	t: |s: |d: C:☐ F:○	t: |s: |d: C:☐ F:○	t: |s: |d: C:☐ F:○
68↘ |a:	t: |s: |d: C:☐ F:○	t: |s: |d: C:☐ F:○	t: |s: |d: C:☐ F:○

Movement	Bunkai 1	Bunkai 2	Bunkai 3
69↺ |a:	t: |s: |d: C:☐F:○	t: |s: |d: C:☐F:○	t: |s: |d: C:☐F:○
70↺ |a:	t: |s: |d: C:☐F:○	t: |s: |d: C:☐F:○	t: |s: |d: C:☐F:○
71↺ |a:	t: |s: |d: C:☐F:○	t: |s: |d: C:☐F:○	t: |s: |d: C:☐F:○
72⇨ |a:	t: |s: |d: C:☐F:○	t: |s: |d: C:☐F:○	t: |s: |d: C:☐F:○

Movement	Bunkai 1	Bunkai 2	Bunkai 3
73⇨ |a:	t: |s: |d: C:☐ F:○	t: |s: |d: C:☐ F:○	t: |s: |d: C:☐ F:○
74⇨ |a:	t: |s: |d: C:☐ F:○	t: |s: |d: C:☐ F:○	t: |s: |d: C:☐ F:○
75⇧ |a:	t: |s: |d: C:☐ F:○	t: |s: |d: C:☐ F:○	t: |s: |d: C:☐ F:○
76⇧ |a:	t: |s: |d: C:☐ F:○	t: |s: |d: C:☐ F:○	t: |s: |d: C:☐ F:○

Movement	Bunkai 1	Bunkai 2	Bunkai 3
77⇧ |a:	t: |s: |d: C:☐ F:◯	t: |s: |d: C:☐ F:◯	t: |s: |d: C:☐ F:◯
78⇧ |a:	t: |s: |d: C:☐ F:◯	t: |s: |d: C:☐ F:◯	t: |s: |d: C:☐ F:◯
79⇧ |a:	t: |s: |d: C:☐ F:◯	t: |s: |d: C:☐ F:◯	t: |s: |d: C:☐ F:◯
80⇧ |a:	t: |s: |d: C:☐ F:◯	t: |s: |d: C:☐ F:◯	t: |s: |d: C:☐ F:◯

Movement	Bunkai 1	Bunkai 2	Bunkai 3
81 ⇧ | a:	t: |s: |d: C:☐ F:◯	t: |s: |d: C:☐ F:◯	t: |s: |d: C:☐ F:◯
82⇧ | a:	t: |s: |d: C:☐ F:◯	t: |s: |d: C:☐ F:◯	t: |s: |d: C:☐ F:◯
83⇩ | a:	t: |s: |d: C:☐ F:◯	t: |s: |d: C:☐ F:◯	t: |s: |d: C:☐ F:◯
84⇩ | a:	t: |s: |d: C:☐ F:◯	t: |s: |d: C:☐ F:◯	t: |s: |d: C:☐ F:◯

Movement	Bunkai 1	Bunkai 2	Bunkai 3
85⇩ |a:	t: |s: |d: C:☐ F:◯	t: |s: |d: C:☐ F:◯	t: |s: |d: C:☐ F:◯
86⇩ |a:	t: |s: |d: C:☐ F:◯	t: |s: |d: C:☐ F:◯	t: |s: |d: C:☐ F:◯
87⇩ |a:	t: |s: |d: C:☐ F:◯	t: |s: |d: C:☐ F:◯	t: |s: |d: C:☐ F:◯
88⇩ |a:	t: |s: |d: C:☐ F:◯	t: |s: |d: C:☐ F:◯	t: |s: |d: C:☐ F:◯

Kusanku Breakdown

This section gives a brief explanation of each movement, following the numbering of the photos. Reminder - this is provided for reference only (see Note on page 8).

1. Stand at attention
2. Bow
3. Salutation
4. Press downward
5. Raise arms up...
6. Move arms in large circle...
7. Ending palm up in front of you
8. Hands to guard position
9. Feet out into ready stance
10. Pivot on heels to 45° Seisan stance - high/low block
11. Pivot on heels to 45° Seisan stance - high/low block
12. Left hand side block
13. Left foot stomp
14. Pivot on heels to 45° Seisan stance - right hand punch
15. Right hand side block
16. Right foot stomp
17. Pivot on heels to 45° Seisan stance - left hand punch
18. Left hand side block
19. Draw back 180°, stack hands on left hip
20. Double strike - right hand backfist and right straight kick
21. Turn 180° into left foot forward guard
22. Step up into right foot forward guard
23. Step up into left foot forward guard
24. Step up with right foot, right hand lift ...

25. Right hand punch
26. Turn 180°, left hand punch
27. Step up with right foot, right hand punch
28. Pivot 180° into crane stance, right hand chop out
29. Right foot straight kick
30. Turn 180° into kneeling position, left hand side block
31. Stand up, right hand straight punch
32. Turn feet into crane stance, right hand chop out
33. Right foot straight kick
34. Turn 180° into kneeling position, left hand side block
35. Stand up, right hand straight punch
36. Draw back to your right, facing left. Stack hands on right hip
37. Double strike - left hand backfist and left straight kick
38. Go down on right knee, right elbow smash
39. Draw back 180°, stack hand on left hip
40. Double strike - right hand backfist, right straight kick
41. Go down on left knee, left elbow smash
42. Stand up into guard position on a 45° left
43. Step up with right foot into guard
44. Pivot into guard 45° right
45. Step up with left foot into guard
46. Draw back into Seiunchin stance, chest high x-block
47. Pivot 90° into crane stance, right hand chop out
48. Right foot kick...
49. Set right foot down in front of left foot, left hand hammer smash down
50. Right hand hammer smash down
51. Step out with left foot into Seisan stance, right hand side block
52. Left hand punch
53. Right hand punch
54. Draw back 180°, stack hands on right hip

55. Left hand backfist, open hand
56. Right foot kick into open hand
57. Turn 180°, drop to all fours, right knee up
58. Turn 180°, drop to all fours, left knee up
59. Stand up into right foot forward Seisan stance, right hand side block
60. Left hand punch
61. Right hand punch
62. Draw back 180°, stack hands on right hip
63. Left hand palm up over left leg
64. Turn left hand and push
65. Step up with right leg into crane stance on 45°, right hand gouge
66. Pivot 360° on right foot, left hand leg block
67. Double strike - left hand backfist, left straight kick
68. Right elbow smash into left hand
69. Turn 90 into right foot forward Seisan stance, right hand high left hand low
70. Push out with both hands
71. Squat block, left hand high
72. Pivot 180° into Seiunchin stance, left hand hammer fist low
73. Right hand hammer fist low
74. Chest-high x-block
75. Pivot clockwise 270°, downward x-block
76. Draw back with hand stacked on right hip
77. Double-jump kick, starting with the right...
78. And ending with the left
79. Left foot forward Seisan stance, downward x-block
80. Step up with right foot, right hand side block
81. Left hand punch
82. Right hand punch
83. Turn 180° into left foot forward guard

84. Step up into right foot forward guard
85. Draw feet in to stand at attention
86. Closing salutation
87. Bow
88. End of kata

Sunsu

Kata

Note: Photos were taken at an angle that shows each movement best – refer to arrows for direction faced in that particular movement. See "Note" on page 8.

Movement	Bunkai 1	Bunkai 2	Bunkai 3
1 ⇩ |a:	t: |s: |d: C:☐ F:◯	t: |s: |d: C:☐ F:◯	t: |s: |d: C:☐ F:◯
2 ⇩ |a:	t: |s: |d: C:☐ F:◯	t: |s: |d: C:☐ F:◯	t: |s: |d: C:☐ F:◯
3 ⇩ |a:	t: |s: |d: C:☐ F:◯	t: |s: |d: C:☐ F:◯	t: |s: |d: C:☐ F:◯
4 ⇩ |a:	t: |s: |d: C:☐ F:◯	t: |s: |d: C:☐ F:◯	t: |s: |d: C:☐ F:◯

Movement	Bunkai 1	Bunkai 2	Bunkai 3
5⇩ |a:	t: |s: |d: C:☐ F:○	t: |s: |d: C:☐ F:○	t: |s: |d: C:☐ F:○
6⇩ |a:	t: |s: |d: C:☐ F:○	t: |s: |d: C:☐ F:○	t: |s: |d: C:☐ F:○
7⇩ |a:	t: |s: |d: C:☐ F:○	t: |s: |d: C:☐ F:○	t: |s: |d: C:☐ F:○
8⇩ |a:	t: |s: |d: C:☐ F:○	t: |s: |d: C:☐ F:○	t: |s: |d: C:☐ F:○

Movement	Bunkai 1	Bunkai 2	Bunkai 3
9⇩ |a:	t: |s: |d:	t: |s: |d:	t: |s: |d:
	C:☐ F:◯	C:☐ F:◯	C:☐ F:◯
10⇩ |a:	t: |s: |d:	t: |s: |d:	t: |s: |d:
	C:☐ F:◯	C:☐ F:◯	C:☐ F:◯
11⇩ |a:	t: |s: |d:	t: |s: |d:	t: |s: |d:
	C:☐ F:◯	C:☐ F:◯	C:☐ F:◯
12⇩ |a:	t: |s: |d:	t: |s: |d:	t: |s: |d:
	C:☐ F:◯	C:☐ F:◯	C:☐ F:◯

Movement	Bunkai 1	Bunkai 2	Bunkai 3
13⇩ | a:	t: |s: |d:	t: |s: |d:	t: |s: |d:
	C:☐ F:◯	C:☐ F:◯	C:☐ F:◯
14⇩ | a:	t: |s: |d:	t: |s: |d:	t: |s: |d:
	C:☐ F:◯	C:☐ F:◯	C:☐ F:◯
15⇩ | a:	t: |s: |d:	t: |s: |d:	t: |s: |d:
	C:☐ F:◯	C:☐ F:◯	C:☐ F:◯
16⇩ | a:	t: |s: |d:	t: |s: |d:	t: |s: |d:
	C:☐ F:◯	C:☐ F:◯	C:☐ F:◯

Movement	Bunkai 1	Bunkai 2	Bunkai 3
17⇩ |a:	t: |s: |d: C:☐ F:◯	t: |s: |d: C:☐ F:◯	t: |s: |d: C:☐ F:◯
18⇩ |a:	t: |s: |d: C:☐ F:◯	t: |s: |d: C:☐ F:◯	t: |s: |d: C:☐ F:◯
19⇩ |a:	t: |s: |d: C:☐ F:◯	t: |s: |d: C:☐ F:◯	t: |s: |d: C:☐ F:◯
20⇩ |a:	t: |s: |d: C:☐ F:◯	t: |s: |d: C:☐ F:◯	t: |s: |d: C:☐ F:◯

Movement	Bunkai 1	Bunkai 2	Bunkai 3
21 ⇩ | a:	t: | s: | d: C:☐ F:◯	t: | s: | d: C:☐ F:◯	t: | s: | d: C:☐ F:◯
22 ⇩ | a:	t: | s: | d: C:☐ F:◯	t: | s: | d: C:☐ F:◯	t: | s: | d: C:☐ F:◯
23 ⇩ | a:	t: | s: | d: C:☐ F:◯	t: | s: | d: C:☐ F:◯	t: | s: | d: C:☐ F:◯
24 ⇨ | a:	t: | s: | d: C:☐ F:◯	t: | s: | d: C:☐ F:◯	t: | s: | d: C:☐ F:◯

Movement	Bunkai 1	Bunkai 2	Bunkai 3
25⇧ |a:	t: |s: |d: C:☐ F:○	t: |s: |d: C:☐ F:○	t: |s: |d: C:☐ F:○
26⇧ |a:	t: |s: |d: C:☐ F:○	t: |s: |d: C:☐ F:○	t: |s: |d: C:☐ F:○
27⇧ |a:	t: |s: |d: C:☐ F:○	t: |s: |d: C:☐ F:○	t: |s: |d: C:☐ F:○
28⇩ |a:	t: |s: |d: C:☐ F:○	t: |s: |d: C:☐ F:○	t: |s: |d: C:☐ F:○

Movement	Bunkai 1	Bunkai 2	Bunkai 3
29⇩ |a:	t: |s: |d: c:☐ f:○	t: |s: |d: c:☐ f:○	t: |s: |d: c:☐ f:○
30⇩ |a:	t: |s: |d: c:☐ f:○	t: |s: |d: c:☐ f:○	t: |s: |d: c:☐ f:○
31⇨ |a:	t: |s: |d: c:☐ f:○	t: |s: |d: c:☐ f:○	t: |s: |d: c:☐ f:○
32⇩ |a:	t: |s: |d: c:☐ f:○	t: |s: |d: c:☐ f:○	t: |s: |d: c:☐ f:○

Movement	Bunkai 1	Bunkai 2	Bunkai 3
33⇐ |a:	t: |s: |d:	t: |s: |d:	t: |s: |d:
	C:☐ F:◯	C:☐ F:◯	C:☐ F:◯
34⇓ |a:	t: |s: |d:	t: |s: |d:	t: |s: |d:
	C:☐ F:◯	C:☐ F:◯	C:☐ F:◯
35⇓ |a:	t: |s: |d:	t: |s: |d:	t: |s: |d:
	C:☐ F:◯	C:☐ F:◯	C:☐ F:◯
36⇓ |a:	t: |s: |d:	t: |s: |d:	t: |s: |d:
	C:☐ F:◯	C:☐ F:◯	C:☐ F:◯

Movement	Bunkai 1	Bunkai 2	Bunkai 3
37⇩ |a:	t: |s: |d: C:☐F:◯	t: |s: |d: C:☐F:◯	t: |s: |d: C:☐F:◯
38⇧ |a:	t: |s: |d: C:☐F:◯	t: |s: |d: C:☐F:◯	t: |s: |d: C:☐F:◯
39⇧ |a:	t: |s: |d: C:☐F:◯	t: |s: |d: C:☐F:◯	t: |s: |d: C:☐F:◯
40⇧ |a:	t: |s: |d: C:☐F:◯	t: |s: |d: C:☐F:◯	t: |s: |d: C:☐F:◯

Movement	Bunkai 1	Bunkai 2	Bunkai 3
41 ⇧ │a:	t: │s: │d:	t: │s: │d:	t: │s: │d:
	C:☐F:◯	C:☐F:◯	C:☐F:◯
42 ⇧ │a:	t: │s: │d:	t: │s: │d:	t: │s: │d:
	C:☐F:◯	C:☐F:◯	C:☐F:◯
43 ⇧ │a:	t: │s: │d:	t: │s: │d:	t: │s: │d:
	C:☐F:◯	C:☐F:◯	C:☐F:◯
44 ⇧ │a:	t: │s: │d:	t: │s: │d:	t: │s: │d:
	C:☐F:◯	C:☐F:◯	C:☐F:◯

Movement	Bunkai 1	Bunkai 2	Bunkai 3
45⇩ |a:	t: |s: |d: C:☐ F:◯	t: |s: |d: C:☐ F:◯	t: |s: |d: C:☐ F:◯
46⇩ |a:	t: |s: |d: C:☐ F:◯	t: |s: |d: C:☐ F:◯	t: |s: |d: C:☐ F:◯
47⇩ |a:	t: |s: |d: C:☐ F:◯	t: |s: |d: C:☐ F:◯	t: |s: |d: C:☐ F:◯
48⇩ |a:	t: |s: |d: C:☐ F:◯	t: |s: |d: C:☐ F:◯	t: |s: |d: C:☐ F:◯

Movement	Bunkai 1	Bunkai 2	Bunkai 3
49⇩ |a:	t: |s: |d:	t: |s: |d:	t: |s: |d:
	C:☐F:◯	C:☐F:◯	C:☐F:◯
50⇩ |a:	t: |s: |d:	t: |s: |d:	t: |s: |d:
	C:☐F:◯	C:☐F:◯	C:☐F:◯
51⇩ |a:	t: |s: |d:	t: |s: |d:	t: |s: |d:
	C:☐F:◯	C:☐F:◯	C:☐F:◯
52⇩ |a:	t: |s: |d:	t: |s: |d:	t: |s: |d:
	C:☐F:◯	C:☐F:◯	C:☐F:◯

Movement	Bunkai 1	Bunkai 2	Bunkai 3
53⇩ |a:	t: |s: |d: C:☐ F:◯	t: |s: |d: C:☐ F:◯	t: |s: |d: C:☐ F:◯
54⇩ |a:	t: |s: |d: C:☐ F:◯	t: |s: |d: C:☐ F:◯	t: |s: |d: C:☐ F:◯
55⇩ |a:	t: |s: |d: C:☐ F:◯	t: |s: |d: C:☐ F:◯	t: |s: |d: C:☐ F:◯
56⇩ |a:	t: |s: |d: C:☐ F:◯	t: |s: |d: C:☐ F:◯	t: |s: |d: C:☐ F:◯

Bunkai Notebook - Isshinryu

Movement	Bunkai 1	Bunkai 2	Bunkai 3
57⇩ |a:	t: |s: |d: C:☐ F:◯	t: |s: |d: C:☐ F:◯	t: |s: |d: C:☐ F:◯
58⇐ |a:	t: |s: |d: C:☐ F:◯	t: |s: |d: C:☐ F:◯	t: |s: |d: C:☐ F:◯
59⇐ |a:	t: |s: |d: C:☐ F:◯	t: |s: |d: C:☐ F:◯	t: |s: |d: C:☐ F:◯
60⇐ |a:	t: |s: |d: C:☐ F:◯	t: |s: |d: C:☐ F:◯	t: |s: |d: C:☐ F:◯

Movement	Bunkai 1	Bunkai 2	Bunkai 3
61 ⇦ |a:	t: |s: |d: C:☐F:◯	t: |s: |d: C:☐F:◯	t: |s: |d: C:☐F:◯
62⇨ |a:	t: |s: |d: C:☐F:◯	t: |s: |d: C:☐F:◯	t: |s: |d: C:☐F:◯
63⇨ |a:	t: |s: |d: C:☐F:◯	t: |s: |d: C:☐F:◯	t: |s: |d: C:☐F:◯
64⇨ |a:	t: |s: |d: C:☐F:◯	t: |s: |d: C:☐F:◯	t: |s: |d: C:☐F:◯

Movement	Bunkai 1	Bunkai 2	Bunkai 3
65⇨ |a:	t: |s: |d: C:☐ F:◯	t: |s: |d: C:☐ F:◯	t: |s: |d: C:☐ F:◯
66⇧ |a:	t: |s: |d: C:☐ F:◯	t: |s: |d: C:☐ F:◯	t: |s: |d: C:☐ F:◯
67⇧ |a:	t: |s: |d: C:☐ F:◯	t: |s: |d: C:☐ F:◯	t: |s: |d: C:☐ F:◯
68⇧ |a:	t: |s: |d: C:☐ F:◯	t: |s: |d: C:☐ F:◯	t: |s: |d: C:☐ F:◯

Movement	Bunkai 1	Bunkai 2	Bunkai 3
69⇧ |a:	t: |s: |d: C:☐ F:◯	t: |s: |d: C:☐ F:◯	t: |s: |d: C:☐ F:◯
70⇩ |a:	t: |s: |d: C:☐ F:◯	t: |s: |d: C:☐ F:◯	t: |s: |d: C:☐ F:◯
71⇩ |a:	t: |s: |d: C:☐ F:◯	t: |s: |d: C:☐ F:◯	t: |s: |d: C:☐ F:◯
72⇩ |a:	t: |s: |d: C:☐ F:◯	t: |s: |d: C:☐ F:◯	t: |s: |d: C:☐ F:◯

Movement	Bunkai 1	Bunkai 2	Bunkai 3
73⇩ |a:	t: |s: |d: C:☐F:○	t: |s: |d: C:☐F:○	t: |s: |d: C:☐F:○
74⇩ |a:	t: |s: |d: C:☐F:○	t: |s: |d: C:☐F:○	t: |s: |d: C:☐F:○
75⇨ |a:	t: |s: |d: C:☐F:○	t: |s: |d: C:☐F:○	t: |s: |d: C:☐F:○
76↘ |a:	t: |s: |d: C:☐F:○	t: |s: |d: C:☐F:○	t: |s: |d: C:☐F:○

Movement	Bunkai 1	Bunkai 2	Bunkai 3
77 ↘ |a:	t: |s: |d: C:☐ F:◯	t: |s: |d: C:☐ F:◯	t: |s: |d: C:☐ F:◯
78 ↘ |a:	t: |s: |d: C:☐ F:◯	t: |s: |d: C:☐ F:◯	t: |s: |d: C:☐ F:◯
79 ↘ |a:	t: |s: |d: C:☐ F:◯	t: |s: |d: C:☐ F:◯	t: |s: |d: C:☐ F:◯
80 ⇨ |a:	t: |s: |d: C:☐ F:◯	t: |s: |d: C:☐ F:◯	t: |s: |d: C:☐ F:◯

Movement	Bunkai 1	Bunkai 2	Bunkai 3
81 ⇨ |a:	t: |s: |d: C:☐F:○	t: |s: |d: C:☐F:○	t: |s: |d: C:☐F:○
82⇨ |a:	t: |s: |d: C:☐F:○	t: |s: |d: C:☐F:○	t: |s: |d: C:☐F:○
83⇨ |a:	t: |s: |d: C:☐F:○	t: |s: |d: C:☐F:○	t: |s: |d: C:☐F:○
84⇦ |a:	t: |s: |d: C:☐F:○	t: |s: |d: C:☐F:○	t: |s: |d: C:☐F:○

Movement	Bunkai 1	Bunkai 2	Bunkai 3
85⇐ |a:	t: |s: |d: C:☐ F:◯	t: |s: |d: C:☐ F:◯	t: |s: |d: C:☐ F:◯
86⇐ |a:	t: |s: |d: C:☐ F:◯	t: |s: |d: C:☐ F:◯	t: |s: |d: C:☐ F:◯
87⇐ |a:	t: |s: |d: C:☐ F:◯	t: |s: |d: C:☐ F:◯	t: |s: |d: C:☐ F:◯
88↘ |a:	t: |s: |d: C:☐ F:◯	t: |s: |d: C:☐ F:◯	t: |s: |d: C:☐ F:◯

Movement	Bunkai 1	Bunkai 2	Bunkai 3
89↖ |a:	t: |s: |d: C:☐F:○	t: |s: |d: C:☐F:○	t: |s: |d: C:☐F:○
90⇩ |a:	t: |s: |d: C:☐F:○	t: |s: |d: C:☐F:○	t: |s: |d: C:☐F:○
91⇩ |a:	t: |s: |d: C:☐F:○	t: |s: |d: C:☐F:○	t: |s: |d: C:☐F:○
92⇩ |a:	t: |s: |d: C:☐F:○	t: |s: |d: C:☐F:○	t: |s: |d: C:☐F:○

Movement	Bunkai 1	Bunkai 2	Bunkai 3
93⇩ |a:	t: |s: |d:	t: |s: |d:	t: |s: |d:
	C:☐ F:◯	C:☐ F:◯	C:☐ F:◯
94⇩ |a:	t: |s: |d:	t: |s: |d:	t: |s: |d:
	C:☐ F:◯	C:☐ F:◯	C:☐ F:◯
95⇩ |a:	t: |s: |d:	t: |s: |d:	t: |s: |d:
	C:☐ F:◯	C:☐ F:◯	C:☐ F:◯
96⇩ |a:	t: |s: |d:	t: |s: |d:	t: |s: |d:
	C:☐ F:◯	C:☐ F:◯	C:☐ F:◯

Movement	Bunkai 1	Bunkai 2	Bunkai 3
97⇩ |a:	t: |s: |d: C:☐F:○	t: |s: |d: C:☐F:○	t: |s: |d: C:☐F:○
98⇩⇧ |a:	t: |s: |d: C:☐F:○	t: |s: |d: C:☐F:○	t: |s: |d: C:☐F:○
99⇩ |a:	t: |s: |d: C:☐F:○	t: |s: |d: C:☐F:○	t: |s: |d: C:☐F:○

Sunsu Breakdown

This section gives a brief explanation of each movement, following the numbering of the photos. Reminder - this is provided for reference only (see Note on page 8).

1. Stand at attention
2. Bow
3. Salutation
4. Ready stance
5. Left foot forward, hands up
6. Draw back right hand
7. Right hand twist punch
8. Hands back up
9. Step up with right foot, draw back left hand
10. Left hand twist punch
11. Hands back up
12. Step up with left foot, draw back right hand
13. Right hand twist punch
14. Hands back up
15. Hands at hips, shuffle forward
16. Double gouge outward
17. Turn hands over and separate
18. Draw hands back to waist
19. Double gouge outward
20. Turn hands over and separate
21. Step back with left foot, right hand side block
22. Left hand punch
23. Right hand punch
24. Turn left 90° into Seiunchin stance, both hands high
25. Pivot left 90°, left hand chop
26. Right hand chop
27. Left hand gouge over right hand

28. Pivot 180°, right hand open arc sweep
29. Left hand gouge
30. Stack hands on right hip
31. Left side kick
32. Stack hands on left hip
33. Right side kick
34. Left foot forward guard
35. Step up with right foot, right hand gouge
36. Shuffle forward, left hand gouge
37. Right hand gouge
38. Draw back 180°, stack hands on right hip
39. Left hand backfist
40. Draw left hand to forehead, right hand chop out
41. Right foot straight kick
42. Right hand leg block
43. Switch hands low/high
44. Switch hands high/low
45. Turn 180° into left foot forward guard
46. Angle body to the left
47. Right foot forward on angle kick
48. Right foot forward Seisan stance, hands on hips
49. Double punch, left hand high
50. Step up with left foot, hands on hips
51. Double punch, right hand high
52. Draw back into cat stance, fist in front of face
53. Double break upwards
54. Step out with right foot, stack hands on right hip
55. Left foot roundhouse kick
56. Stack hands on left hip
57. Right foot roundhouse kick
58. Turn 90° to the right, gouge with left hand
59. Right elbow strike
60. Left elbow strike

61. Right elbow strike
62. Turn 180°, gouge with right hand
63. Left elbow strike
64. Right elbow strike
65. Left elbow strike
66. Turn 90° to the left into guard
67. Step up, right elbow strike
68. Left elbow strike
69. Right elbow strike
70. Turn 180°, left hand over left leg
71. Step up with right foot, right hand lift
72. Pivot 180° on right heel, left elbow strike
73. Draw back into cat stance, right hand at head, left hand low
74. Set left foot out into Seiunchin stance, close hands
75. Pivot 180°, left hand push down
76. Right elbow block
77. Right hand backfist
78. Step across with left foot, both hands gouge low
79. Close hands, Right foot side kick
80. Lift up with right hand
81. Palm heel strike with left hand
82. Right knee strike
83. Right hand punch
84. Turn 180°, left hand lift
85. Right hand palm heel strike
86. Left knee strike
87. Left hand punch
88. Step back 90° to right into crane stance, high/low block
89. Right foot straight kick
90. Turn to front in crane stance, high/low block
91. Left foot straight kick
92. Left foot forward guard position

93. Step up with right foot, left hand over right
94. Rotate to right hand over left
95. Pull downward
96. Bring feet together to stand at attention
97. Closing salutation
98. Bow
99. End of kata

Sanchin Kata

Note: Photos were taken at an angle that shows each movement best – refer to arrows for direction faced in that particular movement. See "Note" on page 8.

Movement	Bunkai 1	Bunkai 2	Bunkai 3
1 ⇩ |a:	t: |s: |d: C:☐F:○	t: |s: |d: C:☐F:○	t: |s: |d: C:☐F:○
2⇩ |a:	t: |s: |d: C:☐F:○	t: |s: |d: C:☐F:○	t: |s: |d: C:☐F:○
3⇩ |a:	t: |s: |d: C:☐F:○	t: |s: |d: C:☐F:○	t: |s: |d: C:☐F:○
4⇩ |a:	t: |s: |d: C:☐F:○	t: |s: |d: C:☐F:○	t: |s: |d: C:☐F:○

Movement	Bunkai 1	Bunkai 2	Bunkai 3
5⇩ |a:	t: |s: |d: C:☐ F:○	t: |s: |d: C:☐ F:○	t: |s: |d: C:☐ F:○
6⇩ |a:	t: |s: |d: C:☐ F:○	t: |s: |d: C:☐ F:○	t: |s: |d: C:☐ F:○
7⇩ |a:	t: |s: |d: C:☐ F:○	t: |s: |d: C:☐ F:○	t: |s: |d: C:☐ F:○
8⇩ |a:	t: |s: |d: C:☐ F:○	t: |s: |d: C:☐ F:○	t: |s: |d: C:☐ F:○

Movement	Bunkai 1	Bunkai 2	Bunkai 3
9⇓ |a:	t: |s: |d: C:☐ F:○	t: |s: |d: C:☐ F:○	t: |s: |d: C:☐ F:○
10⇓ |a:	t: |s: |d: C:☐ F:○	t: |s: |d: C:☐ F:○	t: |s: |d: C:☐ F:○
11⇓ |a:	t: |s: |d: C:☐ F:○	t: |s: |d: C:☐ F:○	t: |s: |d: C:☐ F:○
12⇓ |a:	t: |s: |d: C:☐ F:○	t: |s: |d: C:☐ F:○	t: |s: |d: C:☐ F:○

Movement	Bunkai 1	Bunkai 2	Bunkai 3
13⇩ |a:	t: |s: |d: C:☐ F:◯	t: |s: |d: C:☐ F:◯	t: |s: |d: C:☐ F:◯
14⇩ |a:	t: |s: |d: C:☐ F:◯	t: |s: |d: C:☐ F:◯	t: |s: |d: C:☐ F:◯
15⇩ |a:	t: |s: |d: C:☐ F:◯	t: |s: |d: C:☐ F:◯	t: |s: |d: C:☐ F:◯
16⇩ |a:	t: |s: |d: C:☐ F:◯	t: |s: |d: C:☐ F:◯	t: |s: |d: C:☐ F:◯

Movement	Bunkai 1	Bunkai 2	Bunkai 3
17⇩ | a:	t: |s: |d: C:☐ F:◯	t: |s: |d: C:☐ F:◯	t: |s: |d: C:☐ F:◯
18⇩ | a:	t: |s: |d: C:☐ F:◯	t: |s: |d: C:☐ F:◯	t: |s: |d: C:☐ F:◯
19⇩ | a:	t: |s: |d: C:☐ F:◯	t: |s: |d: C:☐ F:◯	t: |s: |d: C:☐ F:◯
20⇩ | a:	t: |s: |d: C:☐ F:◯	t: |s: |d: C:☐ F:◯	t: |s: |d: C:☐ F:◯

Movement	Bunkai 1	Bunkai 2	Bunkai 3
21 ⇩ | a:	t: | s: | d: C:☐ F:○	t: | s: | d: C:☐ F:○	t: | s: | d: C:☐ F:○
22⇩ | a:	t: | s: | d: C:☐ F:○	t: | s: | d: C:☐ F:○	t: | s: | d: C:☐ F:○
23⇩ | a:	t: | s: | d: C:☐ F:○	t: | s: | d: C:☐ F:○	t: | s: | d: C:☐ F:○
24⇩ | a:	t: | s: | d: C:☐ F:○	t: | s: | d: C:☐ F:○	t: | s: | d: C:☐ F:○

Movement	Bunkai 1	Bunkai 2	Bunkai 3
25⇩ | a:	t: | s: | d: C:☐ F:◯	t: | s: | d: C:☐ F:◯	t: | s: | d: C:☐ F:◯
26⇩ | a:	t: | s: | d: C:☐ F:◯	t: | s: | d: C:☐ F:◯	t: | s: | d: C:☐ F:◯
27⇩ | a:	t: | s: | d: C:☐ F:◯	t: | s: | d: C:☐ F:◯	t: | s: | d: C:☐ F:◯
28⇩ | a:	t: | s: | d: C:☐ F:◯	t: | s: | d: C:☐ F:◯	t: | s: | d: C:☐ F:◯

Movement	Bunkai 1	Bunkai 2	Bunkai 3
29⇩ |a:	t: |s: |d: C:☐ F:○	t: |s: |d: C:☐ F:○	t: |s: |d: C:☐ F:○
30⇩ |a:	t: |s: |d: C:☐ F:○	t: |s: |d: C:☐ F:○	t: |s: |d: C:☐ F:○
31⇩ |a:	t: |s: |d: C:☐ F:○	t: |s: |d: C:☐ F:○	t: |s: |d: C:☐ F:○
32⇩ |a:	t: |s: |d: C:☐ F:○	t: |s: |d: C:☐ F:○	t: |s: |d: C:☐ F:○

Movement	Bunkai 1	Bunkai 2	Bunkai 3
33⇩ |a:	t: |s: |d:	t: |s: |d:	t: |s: |d:
	C:☐F:○	C:☐F:○	C:☐F:○
34⇩ |a:	t: |s: |d:	t: |s: |d:	t: |s: |d:
	C:☐F:○	C:☐F:○	C:☐F:○
35⇩ |a:	t: |s: |d:	t: |s: |d:	t: |s: |d:
	C:☐F:○	C:☐F:○	C:☐F:○
36⇩ |a:	t: |s: |d:	t: |s: |d:	t: |s: |d:
	C:☐F:○	C:☐F:○	C:☐F:○

Movement	Bunkai 1	Bunkai 2	Bunkai 3
37⇩ |a:	t: |s: |d: C:☐ F:◯	t: |s: |d: C:☐ F:◯	t: |s: |d: C:☐ F:◯
38⇩ |a:	t: |s: |d: C:☐ F:◯	t: |s: |d: C:☐ F:◯	t: |s: |d: C:☐ F:◯
39⇩ |a:	t: |s: |d: C:☐ F:◯	t: |s: |d: C:☐ F:◯	t: |s: |d: C:☐ F:◯
40⇩ |a:	t: |s: |d: C:☐ F:◯	t: |s: |d: C:☐ F:◯	t: |s: |d: C:☐ F:◯

Movement	Bunkai 1	Bunkai 2	Bunkai 3
41 ⇩ |a:	t: |s: |d: C:☐ F:○	t: |s: |d: C:☐ F:○	t: |s: |d: C:☐ F:○
42⇩ |a:	t: |s: |d: C:☐ F:○	t: |s: |d: C:☐ F:○	t: |s: |d: C:☐ F:○
43⇩ |a:	t: |s: |d: C:☐ F:○	t: |s: |d: C:☐ F:○	t: |s: |d: C:☐ F:○
44⇩ |a:	t: |s: |d: C:☐ F:○	t: |s: |d: C:☐ F:○	t: |s: |d: C:☐ F:○

Movement	Bunkai 1	Bunkai 2	Bunkai 3
45⇩ |a:	t: |s: |d: C:☐ F:○	t: |s: |d: C:☐ F:○	t: |s: |d: C:☐ F:○
46⇩ |a:	t: |s: |d: C:☐ F:○	t: |s: |d: C:☐ F:○	t: |s: |d: C:☐ F:○
47⇩ |a:	t: |s: |d: C:☐ F:○	t: |s: |d: C:☐ F:○	t: |s: |d: C:☐ F:○
48⇩ |a:	t: |s: |d: C:☐ F:○	t: |s: |d: C:☐ F:○	t: |s: |d: C:☐ F:○

Movement	Bunkai 1	Bunkai 2	Bunkai 3
49⇩ |a:	t: |s: |d: C:☐ F:◯	t: |s: |d: C:☐ F:◯	t: |s: |d: C:☐ F:◯
50⇩ |a:	t: |s: |d: C:☐ F:◯	t: |s: |d: C:☐ F:◯	t: |s: |d: C:☐ F:◯
51⇩ |a:	t: |s: |d: C:☐ F:◯	t: |s: |d: C:☐ F:◯	t: |s: |d: C:☐ F:◯
52⇩ |a:	t: |s: |d: C:☐ F:◯	t: |s: |d: C:☐ F:◯	t: |s: |d: C:☐ F:◯

Movement	Bunkai 1	Bunkai 2	Bunkai 3
53⇩ |a:	t: |s: |d:	t: |s: |d:	t: |s: |d:
	C:☐F:◯	C:☐F:◯	C:☐F:◯
54⇩ |a:	t: |s: |d:	t: |s: |d:	t: |s: |d:
	C:☐F:◯	C:☐F:◯	C:☐F:◯
55⇩ |a:	t: |s: |d:	t: |s: |d:	t: |s: |d:
	C:☐F:◯	C:☐F:◯	C:☐F:◯

Sanchin Breakdown

This section gives a brief explanation of each movement, following the numbering of the photos. Reminder - this is provided for reference only (see Note on page 8).

1. Stand at attention
2. Bow
3. Salutation
4. Ready stance
5. Step up with right foot, hands up
6. Draw left hand to belt
7. Left hand twist punch
8. Right hand set outward
9. Step up with left foot, both hands up
10. Draw right hand to belt
11. Right hand twist punch
12. Left hand set outward
13. Step up with right foot, both hands up
14. Draw left hand to belt
15. Left hand twist punch
16. Right hand set outward
17. Both hands up
18. Draw right hand to belt
19. Right hand twist punch
20. Left hand set outward
21. Both hands up
22. Draw left hand to belt
23. Left hand twist punch
24. Right hand set outward
25. Both hands open, spread outward
26. Draw both hands up...
27. And back to belt

28. Double gouge outward
29. Turn hands over and separate
30. Draw both hands up...
31. And back to belt
32. Double gouge outward
33. Turn hands over and separate
34. Draw both hands up...
35. And back to belt
36. Double gouge outward
37. Turn hands over and separate
38. Draw both hands up...
39. And back to belt
40. Double gouge outward
41. Turn hands over and separate
42. Backs of hands together, right hand on top
43. Step back with right foot, left hand high right hand low
44. Left hand low, right hand high
45. Double push out
46. Backs of hands together, left hand on top
47. Step back with left foot, right hand high left hand low
48. Right hand low, left hand high
49. Double push out
50. Draw feet together to stand at attention
51. Closing salutation, push down while exhaling
52. Push down while exhaling
53. Push down while exhaling
54. Bow
55. End of kata

APPENDIX A – Additional Bunkai

Use this section when you have more than 3 bunkai for a particular move in a kata and run out of space. Make sure to reference this section in the "a" block above the photo so you remember there are more applications in the back!

Example:

Bunkai 1	Photo #: *3*	Photo #: *4*	Photo #: *5*	Photo #:
Kata: _Seisan_ t: *9* s: *14* d: *2*	*OP is at L side -*	*Reach with RH and grab OP collar*	*Pull OP into LH back fist*	

Additional Bunkai:

Bunkai 1	Photo #:	Photo #:	Photo #:	Photo #:
Kata: _____ t: s: d:				

Bunkai 2	Photo #:	Photo #:	Photo #:	Photo #:
Kata: _____ t: s: d:				

Bunkai Notebook - Isshinryu

Appendix A - Additional Bunkai

Bunkai 3	Photo #:	Photo #:	Photo #:	Photo #:
Kata: _____ t: s: d:				

Bunkai 4	Photo #:	Photo #:	Photo #:	Photo #:
Kata: _____ t: s: d:				

Bunkai 5	Photo #:	Photo #:	Photo #:	Photo #:
Kata: _____ t: s: d:				

Bunkai 6	Photo #:	Photo #:	Photo #:	Photo #:
Kata: _____ t: s: d:				

Appendix A - Additional Bunkai

Bunkai 7	Photo #:	Photo #:	Photo #:	Photo #:
Kata: _____ t: s: d:				

Bunkai 8	Photo #:	Photo #:	Photo #:	Photo #:
Kata: _____ t: s: d:				

Bunkai 9	Photo #:	Photo #:	Photo #:	Photo #:
Kata: _____ t: s: d:				

Bunkai 10	Photo #:	Photo #:	Photo #:	Photo #:
Kata: _____ t: s: d:				

Appendix A - Additional Bunkai

Bunkai 11	Photo #:	Photo #:	Photo #:	Photo #:
Kata: _____ t: s: d:				

Bunkai 12	Photo #:	Photo #:	Photo #:	Photo #:
Kata: _____ t: s: d:				

Bunkai 13	Photo #:	Photo #:	Photo #:	Photo #:
Kata: _____ t: s: d:				

Bunkai 14	Photo #:	Photo #:	Photo #:	Photo #:
Kata: _____ t: s: d:				

Appendix A - Additional Bunkai

Bunkai 15	Photo #:	Photo #:	Photo #:	Photo #:
Kata: _____ t: s: d:				

Bunkai 16	Photo #:	Photo #:	Photo #:	Photo #:
Kata: _____ t: s: d:				

Bunkai 17	Photo #:	Photo #:	Photo #:	Photo #:
Kata: _____ t: s: d:				

Bunkai 18	Photo #:	Photo #:	Photo #:	Photo #:
Kata: _____ t: s: d:				

Bunkai Notebook - Isshinryu

Appendix A - Additional Bunkai

Bunkai 19	Photo #:	Photo #:	Photo #:	Photo #:
Kata: _____ t: s: d:				

Bunkai 20	Photo #:	Photo #:	Photo #:	Photo #:
Kata: _____ t: s: d:				

Bunkai 21	Photo #:	Photo #:	Photo #:	Photo #:
Kata: _____ t: s: d:				

Bunkai 22	Photo #:	Photo #:	Photo #:	Photo #:
Kata: _____ t: s: d:				

Appendix A - Additional Bunkai

Bunkai 23	Photo #:	Photo #:	Photo #:	Photo #:
Kata: ———— t: s: d:				

Bunkai 24	Photo #:	Photo #:	Photo #:	Photo #:
Kata: ———— t: s: d:				

Bunkai 25	Photo #:	Photo #:	Photo #:	Photo #:
Kata: ———— t: s: d:				

Bunkai 26	Photo #:	Photo #:	Photo #:	Photo #:
Kata: ———— t: s: d:				

Appendix A - Additional Bunkai

Bunkai 27	Photo #:	Photo #:	Photo #:	Photo #:
Kata: _____ t: s: d:				

Bunkai 28	Photo #:	Photo #:	Photo #:	Photo #:
Kata: _____ t: s: d:				

Bunkai 29	Photo #:	Photo #:	Photo #:	Photo #:
Kata: _____ t: s: d:				

Bunkai 30	Photo #:	Photo #:	Photo #:	Photo #:
Kata: _____ t: s: d:				

APPENDIX B – Rank record

Use this section to document rank advancements, as well as any critique you received or things to correct by next belt.

Example:

Rank: _*Yellow*___ Date: _*11/23/13*_ Tested by: _*Greg*___

Notes: ___*Need to keep fingers together when I gouge,*

*and make sure to look before I turn.*_____

Rank Record

Rank: _____ Date: _____ Tested by: _____
Notes: _____
_____

Rank: _____ Date: _____ Tested by: _____
Notes: _____
_____

Rank: _____ Date: _____ Tested by: _____
Notes: _____
_____

Rank: _____ Date: _____ Tested by: _____
Notes: _____
_____

Rank: _____ Date: _____ Tested by: _____
Notes: _____
_____

Appendix B – Rank record

Rank: _____ Date: _____ Tested by: _____

Notes: _____

_____

Rank: _____ Date: _____ Tested by: _____

Notes: _____

_____

Rank: _____ Date: _____ Tested by: _____

Notes: _____

_____

Rank: _____ Date: _____ Tested by: _____

Notes: _____

_____

Rank: _____ Date: _____ Tested by: _____

Notes: _____

_____

Rank: _____ Date: _____ Tested by: _____

Notes: _____

_____

Rank: _____ Date: _____ Tested by: _____

Notes: _____

_____

APPENDIX C – Lineage

Use this section to document your school's lineage – who your instructor is, who taught him, all the way back to the original Okinawan masters.

Example:

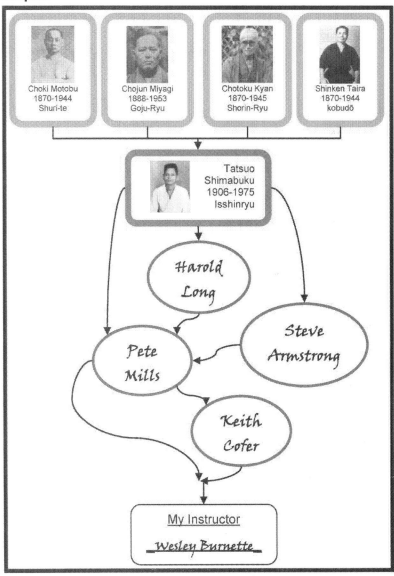

Appendix C - Lineage

Choki Motobu
1870-1944
Shuri-te

Chojun Miyagi
1888-1953
Goju-Ryu

Chotoku Kyan
1870-1945
Shorin-Ryu

Shinken Taira
1870-1944
kobudö

Tatsuo
Shimabuku
1906-1975
Isshinryu

My Instructor

APPENDIX D – Autographs

Use this section to get signatures from famous martial artists at seminars, visiting grandmasters, etc.

_____

Signature

_____   _____   _____

Print name   Date   Location

_____

Signature

_____   _____   _____

Print name   Date   Location

_____

Signature

_____   _____   _____

Print name   Date   Location

_____

Signature

_____   _____   _____

Print name   Date   Location

_____

Signature

_____   _____   _____

Print name   Date   Location

Appendix D – Signatures

Signature

Print name   Date   Location

Signature

Print name   Date   Location

Signature

Print name   Date   Location

Signature

Print name   Date   Location

Signature

Print name   Date   Location

Signature

Print name   Date   Location

APPENDIX E – Notes

Notes

Notes

_____

_____

_____

_____

_____

_____

_____

_____

_____

_____

_____

_____

_____

_____

_____

_____

_____

_____

_____

_____

_____

_____

Appendix E – Notes

Notes

Notes

APPENDIX F – Sources

Use this section to document where you learned a particular bunkai from – just enter your source below and write the reference number in the "s" block when you enter your bunkai.

Examples:
1. _My instructor_
2. _Summer seminar_
3. _Visit from Grandmaster Evan_

Ref. #	Source
1.	
2.	
3.	
4.	
5.	
6.	
7.	
8.	
9.	
10.	
11.	
12.	
13.	
14.	
15.	
16.	

Appendix F - Sources

17. _____

18. _____

19. _____

20. _____

21. _____

22. _____

23. _____

24. _____

25. _____

26. _____

27. _____

28. _____

29. _____

30. _____

31. _____

32. _____

33. _____

34. _____

35. _____

36. _____

37. _____

38. _____

39. _____

40. _____

APPENDIX G – Bunkai Types/Difficulty

Use this section to determine how to fill in the boxes at the start of each bunkai.

Difficulty rating:

1. Easy/Instinctive – No training needed to make effective.
2. Easily mastered – Some training needed to make sure it can be properly applied.
3. Intermediate – Firm knowledge of basic techniques needed before training in this Bunkai.
4. Advanced – Intense training needed or set-up technique required to make opponent more compliant.

Bunkai Types:

Code	Description
D	Self-Defense
C	Compliance technique
G	Grappling Technique
J	Joint lock
K	Killing technique
P	Pressure point
____	_____
____	_____
____	_____
____	_____
____	_____
____	_____

Bunkai Notebook - Isshinryu

APPENDIX H – Abbreviations

This section gives some suggestions for abbreviations to make it faster and easier to jot down Bunkai. Or you can use the blanks provided to create your own.

Abbreviation	Description
B	Back
BF	Backfist
BL	Block
F	Foot
FW	Forward
GB	Grab
H	Hand
K	Kick
L	Left
OP	Opponent
P	Punch
R	Right
T	Turn
UC	Uppercut

~ Coming soon ~

ENCYCLOPEDIA OF BUNAKI
FOR
ISSHINRYU KARATE

The only book with multiple applications for every movement in every kata of the Isshinryu system! Includes step-by-step photos of every Bunkai and kata movement.

$5.00 Off!!!

Submit at least 3 Bunkai to the e-mail address below, and receive a copy of Encyclopedia of Bunaki for Isshinryu Karate at $5 below list price. Bunaki must be submitted by:

1. Written description with reference to kata name and photo #'s used in this journal
2. Filled out pages of this journal scanned into a standard format (PDF, JPG, TIFF)
3. Photo/video demonstration of Bunkai

Be featured!
All who enter will qualify for a discount. If your applications are included in the book, you will be included as a contributor in the book!

BunkaiPress@hotmail.com

Made in the USA
Charleston, SC
09 February 2013